WHEN A CHILD
IS DIFFERENT

WHEN A CHILD IS DIFFERENT

*A Basic Guide for Parents and Friends
of Mentally Retarded Children*

DR. MARIA EGG

Introduction by Eunice Kennedy Shriver

Foreword by Professor J. Lutz, M.D.

LONDON
GEORGE ALLEN & UNWIN LTD
RUSKIN HOUSE MUSEUM STREET

FIRST PUBLISHED IN GREAT BRITAIN IN 1967

This book is copyright under the Berne Convention. Apart from any fair dealing for the purpose of private study, research, criticism or review, as permitted under the Copyright Act, 1956, no portion may be reproduced by any process without written permission. Enquiries should be addressed to the publishers

© 1964 by The John Day Company, Inc.

Translated from the German *Ein Kind Ist Anders*, © 1960
By Guggenbuehl & Huber Schweizer Spiegel Verlag, Zurich

PRINTED IN GREAT BRITAIN
BY PHOTOLITHOGRAPHY
UNWIN BROTHERS LIMITED
WOKING AND LONDON

Contents

Introduction

by

EUNICE KENNEDY SHRIVER

Consultant, President's Panel on Mental Retardation, and Executive
Vice-President, the Joseph P. Kennedy Jr. Foundation

Dear Parents:

*For some time you have been noticing . . . that your
child is in some respects "different" from other children . . . he does not smile at you . . . he does not try
to grasp things you are offering him . . . he does not
kick his legs . . . perhaps he has fallen behind in all
those cute little things babies do . . . perhaps his behavior is . . . different from that of other children of
the same age. . . .*

With these words and with the most tender solicitude,
Maria Egg opens a chapter of her guidebook, designed to
lead parents and their retarded children out of the shadows
of despair and hopelessness into the bright new world of
character formation, good habits, charm and personality
—into the normal world of pride in the child as a precious
member of the family.

9

Sentence after sentence, paragraph after paragraph, there is heart and wisdom, understanding and acceptance, in this book. But not these passive virtues alone. More, there is advice and persuasion; there is help—real help. The reader knows that Dr. Egg has been there, has seen the child and then sat down to talk with the mother (and, I hope, with the father too!). There is acceptance coupled with challenge, compassion with discipline, understanding with sensible suggestions for what to do, specifically—say, after breakfast on Tuesday morning.

It is this practical aspect of the book based on her vast and unequaled experience with retarded children that makes Maria Egg's guidebook for parents the most appealing, the most persuasive, the most helpful, the clearest book about exceptional children ever to appear in the English language. May her name soon become as famous as Dr. Benjamin Spock's!

The publication in English of Dr. Egg's classic work has arrived at the moment of truth for retarded children in the United States. Our country is experiencing an unprecedented surge of interest in the retarded. Medical breakthroughs are occurring rapidly. New discoveries have been made in educational, psychological, and social welfare fields. But it is still a tragedy that mothers and fathers often do not get the vital, new information. Too often and for too long, this new knowledge stays locked up in research papers, libraries and laboratories, or in the professional's head. But with Maria Egg the log jam has been broken. Parents can now learn, for themselves, what to expect, how to act with their retarded child.

To give every parent some understanding of why such

a tragedy has happened to them, Maria Egg discusses some of the medical causes for mental retardation. She dismisses the old wives' tales of punishment to parents for their sins, drinking habits of the father, or infidelities of the mother.

The parents are reminded that mental retardation can happen to anyone, to any family. She points out to parents that mental retardation occurs in all countries, in all races, among rich and poor, among the high and the lowly. And she discusses these facts with her never-failing compassionate understanding of the sorrow of parents when they discover theirs is a retarded child.

"It will be hard to realize that the dreams you nourished before the child's birth will never become reality . . . Your heart will ache. Do not be ashamed of your tears!" She understands the parents' normal desire to reject this lifelong problem placed upon their shoulders, but she does so with gentle advice on how to deal with the disappointment, even the humiliation. "[Your husband] is far from being a bad father if he is not yet ready to let the men at the office see him with the child. Don't insist that the child be taken along on the office picnic. . . ."

She discusses, too, the problem that worries every family: how will the retarded child affect normal brothers and sisters? Maria Egg recognizes that this is an important problem, but shows there are practical, tried solutions. For example: "The other siblings will be more willing to let the handicapped child take part in their play if they know that the mother will see to it that they can from time to time play by themselves . . ." Or a high school student may be understandably angry at his mother when she picks him up in front of school with his abnormal little brother

sitting in the front seat of the car, so Maria Egg cautions
not to do this.

Dr. Egg places the responsibility for teaching the retarded child squarely upon the parents. She believes that
with perseverance they can teach their children almost to
accomplish miracles. She tells us not only what the children can learn, but how they can be taught step by step,
the simplest task first and then the more difficult. On
speech, for example: "As soon as the child can understand
. . . have [him] . . . imitate [after you] . . . 'bow wow'. . . .
Then . . . have the child imitate . . . the sounds of a railroad train . . . Then . . . have the child blow out candles
or . . . get him to blow a cotton ball across the table . . ."

Or, again, on the problems of drinking and eating she
explains: ". . . if the mother holds the child in her arms
in a slightly reclined position, the child will instinctively
swallow the content of the teaspoon . . . Through practice,
we can get the child to the point where he can swallow the
liquid from the teaspoon while sitting upright." Again:
"Cups with one handle are not suitable for retarded children." Or if the child cannot readily adapt to the spoon,
she explains from her experience that ". . . we use a spoon
dipped into a little honey or moistened sugar. In this manner, every successful attempt at the same time leads to a
reward."

Page after page, Maria Egg establishes realistic, attainable goals for the mother, telling her how to teach the
child to draw, model clay, walk, use the toilet. Always she
treats the education of the retarded child with great imagination and perception. "If . . . [the] child notices too
few things . . . take him to the window often and point

out the moving cars in the street. If that does not interest him, perhaps you will have more success with a colored flashlight or with a small mirror with which you can make the sunlight dance."

To teach the retarded child to dress and undress is a problem not only for parents but for camp counselors and institutional personnel. ". . . it is much easier to undress than to dress. . . . The retarded child must first be taught the easier operation. . . . When you undress the child, always do it in the same sequence. . . . Practice with clothing that is a little too large for the child. Get your child to help you . . . guide his hand in taking off shoes and socks . . ." To learn to undress, "We need a bag . . . and we put a large hole for the neck in the closed end of the bag and large armholes in the sides. This is our training aid for . . . putting on . . . blouse, coat . . ."

Is it all worthwhile? "Yes," says Maria Egg. "Your efforts will be richly rewarded. There is a world of difference between a well-trained, well-behaved retarded child and a child who was considered hopeless from the beginning and whose progress was given up. No child should ever be given up. It is worthwhile to make every possible effort with any child." Dr. Egg proves that parents themselves will grow if only they will work with their child.

No book, of course, is faultless, including this memorable one, which suffers, for American usage, because of its heavy concentration on family responsibility and too little on community obligations to the retarded. Even if parents have done all Maria Egg suggests, it is still not enough. There must be special education classes in public schools, rehabilitation and workshop programs, recreational programs, volunteer leadership; yet thousands of our communities still do not have such services, and our children and adults suffer.

And what has happened to the fathers of retarded children? Maria Egg gives them very little to do—yet my experience convinces me that interested and dedicated men are essential if the retarded are ever to obtain the physical education, the medical care, the vocational training, and the jobs necessary to make them productive, self-respecting members of our society.

But these omissions are small matters when measured against Dr. Egg's great achievement in humanizing the problems of the retarded and making so clear the encouraging possibilities for their rehabilitation, education, and employment.

In a memorable passage, Dr. Egg has written:

The blind had their Helen Keller . . . the deaf had Beethoven. . . . Among the retarded there is none who, through his achievements, could demonstrate to the public his value and the value of those similarly afflicted. It is up to us, then, to uphold the value of these human beings. It is up to us to help extend respect for human dignity to these creatures also. It is up to us who live with them and who love them. We know what they need and what they can give us.

True it is, the mentally retarded may never produce a luminous leader personally sharing their disability as Helen Keller shared the blindness of the blind. Yet in Maria Egg the mentally retarded already possess a precious and noble example in the tradition of the Good Samaritan, a person who, having much, has shared her all with those who have no special claim on her mind, heart, and soul. In doing so, Maria Egg has heeded the injunction of the Lord: "Whatever you do for these the least of my children, you do unto Me."

Except for death could there be a greater proof of her love for her fellow man?

Foreword

The problem of mental retardation has manifested itself in various forms over the past several decades; 2 percent of the population (and as much as 3 to 4 percent, if our sampling survey is more extensive) is retarded in mental and psychological development. These individuals have been treated in various ways: some have always been cared for and protected lovingly; others are looked at askance as noisome and useless mouths that must be fed; still others are given employment and assigned to simple jobs when business is good. Most of these individuals learn to walk, talk, and think rather late; they are intellectually and emotionally behind the others when the time comes to place them in kindergarten or school; in most cases, they leave school because they have had to repeat grades once or several times; or they become special cases, provided they are at all suited for school education. Not only are they limited in their ultimate achievements; the development of such capabilities as they may have is so heavily encumbered that they require special assistance from earliest childhood. This assistance must be adapted both to the limitations and especially to the peculiarities of these children. It would be wrong to think that the mentally retarded child need be expected to assimilate simply 50 percent of the subject matter assigned to normal children. The important thing here is not the quantity of subject matter, but the quality of training.

The mentally retarded child, however, is a problem not only for the school but also for the parents. The latter need regular indoctrination in the form of home education training and therapy if they are to do everything they can for the child and if they are to develop the proper attitude toward the fact that one of their children is mentally retarded. This book shows the way; the text is clear and the presentation is well thought out and therefore convincing; based on simple religious faith, it approaches the subject with warm compassion and confidence. It offers fertile soil for the growth of our ideas on the special educational treatment of the retarded, and may well help many dejected parents cast aside their despairing lethargy and begin to stand by their retarded children, ready and able to help.

PROFESSOR J. LUTZ, M.D.
Director,
Psychiatric Polyclinic for
Children and Teenagers,
Zurich

WHEN A CHILD
IS DIFFERENT

1

As the Child Begins to Grow

We ALL KNOW how helpless a newborn infant is. It shows no interest in its surroundings; it does not understand what we say to it; it cannot speak. At birth, the human infant is much more helpless than many a newborn animal. Yet all essential developmental factors are present. The infant has its organs: it has eyes, hands, legs, and ears. But it cannot use them. We need not teach it how to use its limbs: if the child is healthy, it begins to use its organs quite by itself.

It is a marvelous adventure to observe how the infant discovers new things each day.

Soon after birth, the healthy baby can get its milk from the breast or from the bottle: it can suck and even swallow.

Its eyes do not look, as yet; even when its eyes are open, the infant does not see what goes on in its surroundings. Only after several weeks have passed do the eyes follow a shiny or illuminated object. About the second or third month, it begins to look at people who bend over it; and then it gives the mother its first smile. At five or six months, it can even distinguish between Mother and strangers; it begins to react to strangers. When a stranger gets too near it, the infant may show that it does not particularly like him or her.

The newborn also cannot use its limbs too well. It kicks because it's fun to kick; that is the only purpose at the time. After barely a month has passed, the infant manages to find its mouth with its thumb: it begins to suck its thumb. By about the third month, it begins to reach for things that are pleasing; it discovers its hands; it keeps looking at them, contemplating them; gleefully, it plays with its fingers and toes. One or two months later, the infant manages to grasp something and move it to its mouth. Now its hands explore the mother's face, its own body, and anything else it can reach. Somewhat later, the baby starts using both hands in grasping its toys. It can also transfer them from one hand to the other. It begins to raise its head and turn around. During the second six months of its life, it tries to sit up. Toward the end of the first year, the baby tries to pull himself up by the side of the crib; soon he can stand all by himself, and around his first birthday he delights his parents by taking his first steps.

The child's limbs become more and more skilled and its mind develops, too, because the brain is growing. In the newborn, only those parts of the brain are developed which regulate bodily functions—that is to say, heart activity, breathing, digestion, etc. All other parts, such as those we need for thinking, speaking, and decision-making, are still undeveloped. This is why we cannot determine whether a newborn infant is intelligent and what it will develop into.

But we soon notice the gradual awakening of its mind; from this we conclude that its brain is developing. Now the child can recall things that happened earlier. Soon he begins to notice when his meal or his bath is being prepared and expresses joy at these events.

The baby's interest in its environment keeps growing; his life space grows bigger and bigger. Moved from the crib to the playpen, he can see more and more. Once he begins to crawl around, he tries to explore his environment further; he learns by touching things, by handling them again and again. He wants to try and test and reconnoiter everything.

And the child increasingly participates in the life of his family. During the second year, his daily routine is more and more brought in line with that of the grownups. His behavior must also gradually adapt itself to the demands of other people. The infant must satisfy his needs at the proper time and in the proper manner. This creates difficulties in any child. Anyone who has anything to do with children knows that the transition from baby to small child is often quite difficult, both for the mother and for the child.

Life is made for healthy, well-developed children. Society demands that the child meet certain basic requirements if he wants to share in the life of the group. Society demands a standard, a norm. Hence the term "abnormal" or nonstandard for any behavior and any capability that does not fit into this standard pattern.

During the second year, the mother can tell whether the child is adjusting to everyday routine requirements the way he should—the way the norm says he should—or whether there is some ingredient that is not normal. This book is addressed to the parents of those children who are different from others.

2

Our Child Is Different

DEAR PARENTS: For some time you have been noticing on various occasions that your child is in some respects "different" from other children. Perhaps he is "too good"; he lies in his crib indifferently; he does not smile at you; he does not try to grasp things you are offering him; he does not kick his legs. Or he notices things, colors, and sounds—which really should interest him—in a rather hesitant fashion, without any real interest. Or perhaps he has fallen behind in all those cute little things babies do. And perhaps his behavior is in some way noticeably different from that of other children of the same age. Maybe he is always ill-tempered, constantly whining; somehow he makes an unhappy impression in contrast to the healthy babies who peacefully enjoy their young lives and squeal gleefully. Perhaps he moves in an oddly jerky manner. Maybe he does not try to sit up at an age when other children manage to sit. Perhaps he is finding it difficult to learn to walk, or maybe he walks unlike other children: he may have a rolling gait or he may walk on his toes or in

some such strange manner. Perhaps he is not making progress in his speech: he may stutter or speak a few barely
understandable words at a time when other children of
the same age chatter in such a way that even people outside
their own families can understand.

If you have observed these and similar phenomena, it is
time for you to take your child to a doctor. It may be that
some hidden illness or physical deformity is preventing
your child from developing like other children. This may
be the case even when the little one looks "in the pink"
and really healthy.

Perhaps the child is not smiling at you because he does
not see you, though his eyes may be clear.

It may be that your child is not making progress with
his speech because he does not hear your speech at all—or
at least, not correctly. There are children (and adults, for
that matter) who are hard of hearing and who can hear
the slamming of a door or the ringing of a phone, but
perceive human speech only in a distorted fashion.

Your child may move around peculiarly because he is
paralyzed. Not every paralysis manifests itself in a limply
hanging leg or arm. There are paralyses that start from the
brain and affect all movements to a more or less pronounced degree. Thus it happens that some babies cannot
move their limbs freely because they are convulsed and
rigid.

Only the experienced physician can tell whether your
child has some kind of physical irregularity.

The doctor may find that your child has healthy eyes,
healthy ears, and healthy limbs. The difference, compared
to other children, stems from the fact that his brain has

not developed normally and that therefore his mind did not develop properly. Since movements are controlled by the brain, these children often move rather awkwardly, though their limbs may be healthy. The specialist will then tell you that your child is "dull" or "retarded."

3

What Does Mental Retardation Mean?

MENTAL RETARDATION means that your child's brain is developing more slowly than that of other children. As a consequence, the development of the child's entire intellectual life lags behind—his intelligence, his thinking, willing, emotions, as well as dexterity of movement and everything connected with it.

Often the glands are not working the way they should; this serves to retard development further. In many children, disorders in the brain also affect the body: they become cross-eyed or are handicapped in their movements or their growth has been stunted or they look awkward. This applies especially in the case of the so-called "Mongoloids." *But outward appearance is no yardstick for intelligence.* We can find well-informed, pretty, and even beautiful children among the mentally retarded—children whose condition cannot be detected from their outward appearance.

The psychic life of these children is not in line with their age. Here we find children who, at the age of six, behave like three-year-olds. Unfortunately we must not indulge in the hope that they will be as far along as a normal six-year-old after three years have passed (*i.e.*, at the age of nine). The mentally retarded child develops much more slowly than that; the difference between him and the normal child grows as both advance in age.

At the age of fifteen—when other children have completed their schooling and enter vocational training—this child will be on the mental and emotional level of a seven- or eight-year-old. As we know, every young person stops growing roughly around the age of eighteen; by then the development of the brain is essentially completed. The retarded child in our example here may then be on the mental level of a nine- or ten-year-old. He or she will probably look like a young man or like a grown daughter and possibly even be well shaped and nice to look at. It is also possible that he or she may have learned how to behave like a grownup. Still, this individual will be able to cope only with those situations that a nine- or ten-year-old can handle.

Let us assume that an express train and a local train start at the same time. It is obvious that the local train will keep falling behind: the distance between the two trains will keep growing. If we compare the healthy child with the express train, then our mentally retarded are the local trains and often the overland stages

The important thing here is the extent to which development has been slowed. If the child lags but little behind other children of the same age, we speak of "dull or borderline" cases. If the retardation is major in extent, we speak of "mild," "moderate," and "severe" retardation. The most severely involved children are called "profoundly retarded."

The "dull" do not differ greatly from some other children who are still considered normal. As long as they are small, we do not notice anything special about them. In the case of some of them, we do not notice that they can't keep up with their fellows until they start going to school. Most larger communities have special schools or facilities with various names for these children.

We will not be discussing the slightly retarded child in this book; we will concentrate on those whose development is much more limited.

Neither will we be talking about emotionally disturbed children or the so-called hard-to-train children who offer behavior problems. Though the behavior of mentally retarded children offers many problems and their education is not exactly easy, we do not call them "hard to train"; we use this term for those children who cannot adjust to their environment and who are not up to their age level, though they may be as intelligent as the next child. It is difficult to train them because they don't react to their parents and teachers as we would like them to and in a way that is customary. In this book we will take up only those children who are hard to *train* because their mental development is greatly retarded.

4

When You Learn the Truth

WHEN YOU OBSERVE or are told that your child is mentally retarded, it will be little consolation for you to know that you are not the only parents with such a child. In the beginning, you may think that no other parents have been visited by such misfortune. That is why you feel shut out of the group of parents with normal children. Before this child came to you, you probably did not realize that mental retardation can occur in any family, that it is found in all countries, in all races, among rich and poor, among the high and the lowly, among the deeply rooted and among the uprooted, among highly educated and uneducated, and among those we call "just average."

As you begin to notice this you will still say that other families have it easier than you do. If your station in life is high, you will think that simple people find it easier to face the fact that their child is mentally retarded, because they need not set as high goals for their children. If you are among those whose only school was the school of hard knocks, the school of life, then you will say that the "educated" have an easier answer to all the "why's" and "how's" that torment you in connection with your retarded child. If you live in the country, you will think that the people in the city have it easier because there are more opportunities for such children there, more facilities for assistance. And if you live in the city, you will maintain that the retarded child does not stand out as much in a simple rural environment. If you have so far gone through life without religion, you will suppose that religious people have it easier in accepting such a blow of fate. But if you have a faith, then you will say that the faithless find it easier to comprehend all this as a form of "punishment."

The fact is that *all* parents are shocked and shaken when they notice that the child—in whom they have placed such high hopes and for whom they have made such plans—will probably be in need of assistance all its life. It is quite natural for you to refuse to accept this in the beginning— to keep trying to convince yourself and others that the child is healthy. All parents find it difficult to accept the fact that they will not be able to watch their child grow with pride and joy, that he will not be able to compete against or even outstrip his contemporaries. It will be hard to realize that the dreams you nourished before the child's birth will never become reality.

The fact that some children are retarded can be observed immediately after birth. For the parents of these children, this time of supreme bliss is suddenly turned into darkest despair. But in *most* children you cannot notice anything special in the beginning. The baby's physical development may be very good; he may be a sweet, sturdy little child. Only later will the parents become suspicious. Of course, you were afraid of the truth. You did see that your child was not like other children, but you probably told yourself: This is impossible; it'll pass. And as your thoughts ran along these lines you were in the midst of an emotional conflict which is spared no father or mother of a retarded child; this is the struggle between the hope that things are not as you fear they are and the frightening realization that something is indeed wrong. And then came the day when you could no longer shut out reality. You decided to take your child to a doctor or specialist. You made this decision because you saw that your child was in some essential aspects different from what he should be. Nevertheless, you were shaken when the specialist told you what you had been suspecting all along.

Your heart will ache as you are made to see your child's real condition; that is only natural. Do not be ashamed of your tears!

5

How Did It Happen?

ALL PARENTS are tormented by this question when they discover that their child is mentally retarded or when a specialist confirms what they had suspected. Almost always, the first question is: "How did it happen?"

Science does not yet know all the causes of mental retardation. In many cases, not even the best doctor can say where a particular mental disorder came from. For instance, we have no reliable data on the origins of Mongolism.

Away in the back of his or her mind, the parent often has the feeling that he or she shares in the responsibility for the child's condition. Parents seek the fault in themselves or in the spouse. Often the wife reproaches the husband for his behavior during conception, and the husband reproaches the wife for her actions during pregnancy. Such accusations—even when not voiced—can ruin the happiest marriage. They do no one any good. In the vast majority of cases, they do not represent the real cause of the child's debility.

It is fervently to be wished that every father and mother

will shed any guilt feelings they might have and stop all self-accusations. In the vast majority of cases there is no reason to blame the child's infirmity on oneself.

Dear Parents: Unfounded guilt feelings only harm you and your relationship with your child. It is hard to overcome such feelings, but you must keep trying.

Fearfully, most parents ask: "Is it inherited?" We cannot answer this question in every case, but we do know that heredity enters the picture in many cases of mental retardation. The laws of heredity are complicated, and it is not only the dull or borderline parents who are struck by this.

Perhaps you think your child's affliction is connected with certain' illnesses or peculiarities you have observed in your spouse's family. Don't reproach your mate because his father drank or his sister was an immoral woman, because his cousin was hunchbacked or his brother had to attend a special school for slow learners. Your marriage partner had nothing to do with this; besides, all this has no connection with the superiority or inferiority of his inherited disposition. If you should suspect that the sum total of your mate's hereditary factors really has some shortcomings, you must remember that our hereditary predisposition is that part of our being for which we are not responsible. In grown men and women, it should not be their heredity that counts, but what they have done with what they were given.

In addition to heredity, there are other causes of mental retardation, such as certain diseases of the mother during pregnancy, especially German measles. In some cases the blood of the parents is incompatible, and this results in damage to the child. There are also infants whose brains were damaged, for instance during protracted labor or precipitate labor. Various early childhood diseases can also delay mental development considerably, as in the case of encephalitis.

Some children have eclampsia (convulsions) during their first year. This may pass without damage in some; in others it may later turn out that they are mentally retarded. In a particular case, we cannot always be sure whether the child is mentally retarded because he had eclampsia or because his brain was damaged even before.

The correct functioning of the glands is also important in the child's development. When glandular functions are disturbed, the effect may be seen not only in mental development but also in outward appearance. In most cases we cannot tell why certain glands are not working properly.

Often the child's condition is explained by the statement that the mother was frightened by some event during pregnancy or that she had to cope with some great worry or sorrow during that time. We know from experience that this is not true. Emotional shocks of the mother do not cause mental retardation in the child.

Mothers also tend to ascribe the child's mental debility to some insignificant little incident. In most instances, this, too, has no factual basis. When we were children, all of us at one time or another fell out of bed or off a table or ladder, but we are none the worse for it. We and our mothers have long since forgotten the incident. Serious childhood accidents such as skull fractures or brain concussions can of course have grave consequences under certain circumstances.

6

Why?

IT DOES NOT really matter whether or not you find a reason for your child's mental retardation. Even if you did, this would not change anything in your child's condition. Medical explanations do not end the search for an answer. Your heart echoes and re-echoes the question: Why? Why did I have to have such a child? Why do I have to bear this cross?

There is no satisfactory answer. It seems that mental retardation is a part of Creation. For thousands of years we have known that there are mentally retarded people in the world. In the classics, we find that ancient Greeks and Romans had to cope with this problem. It is probably as old as the human race. From this we might well conclude that this condition, too, has its purpose—even though we may not be able to grasp the sense of it in each particular case.

Some parents think that God gave them a retarded child as a punishment because they are not good people. It is generally the deeply religious who have this reaction. But this is not according to what the Bible says. The Gospel of St. John relates that two thousand years ago the Apostles asked Jesus the same question countless parents are still asking Him today.

When a blind man was brought to him, the Disciples asked: "Rabbi, who has sinned, this man or his parents, that he should be born blind?" And Our Saviour replied: "Neither has this man sinned, nor his parents, but the works of God were to be made manifest in him." (John 9: 2-3)

Let all fathers and mothers of retarded children inscribe this sentence in their hearts, for it tells us that this child was not given by way of punishment and that his existence is in keeping with divine law.

The infirm child is no more a punishment for the sins of his parents than the healthy child is a reward for their virtues. We can take no credit when our children are born and remain healthy. This is an unearned gift, a grace. We must accept the life of our children just as we get it from the hand of the Creator. We cannot pick and choose; we cannot know whether the child will have a long or a short life, whether he will blossom or shrink in illness, whether he will walk a straight path or devious byways. This is not easy to accept—either for the parents of handicapped children or for the parents of normal children.

In many cases we can clearly see how much good is done through handicapped children. We can see how an entire family can grow and mature spiritually as it faces the task of caring for an infirm child. How much good is awakened in society as a result of this! At any rate, we could not possibly say which life is valuable and meaningful and which life is worthless and meaningless. It is not for us to judge; we are not equipped to do so.

If you still insist on asking Why, then you must also ask yourself which child can cause more sorrow in the end. It is not always the infirm child. There are healthy children who cause their parents at least as much, if not more, trouble and disgrace—who inflict far worse wounds on their hearts.

In looking at her child's life, every mother, including the mother of a healthy child, sooner or later finds herself in a position where she can only say *"Ecce Ancilla Domini"* —"Behold, I am the servant of the Lord; His will be done." Fortunate are the parents who can say this and mean it; and fortunate is their child, be he healthy or infirm. Out of the knowledge of the wisdom and the goodness of God and out of the belief in the value of each individual soul— no matter how it may be shaped—there can grow a feeling of confidence that will give you strength and make your child happy.

Try not to burden yourselves with confusing questions as to the why and how of things. Do not haggle with fate. Instead of ruminating, try to find ways in which your child can be helped.

7

Is Our Child Curable?

OF COURSE, you will take your child to a good doctor as soon as you notice that he is not developing like other children. The doctor will advise you on how to maintain your child's physical health. If the child has convulsions or seizures, the doctor will prescribe medication to make the seizures stop. If the child is very nervous and "fidgety," he may prescribe tranquilizers in order to make it easier for you to handle the child. If necessary, he can also stimulate glandular activity. Medicine can make many things possible and many others easier. It can stimulate dormant development processes and control those which are not taking place in the proper manner. It can release the child from all kinds of impediments with which many of these children are afflicted, such as enlarged tonsils, anemia, irregularities in metabolism, etc. There are many ways in which an experienced physician can ease the child's lot and further the development of limited predispositions. Thorough medical examination and constant control are therefore integral parts of correct care.

But do not expect the doctor to heal your child's retardation. *No doctor can do that.* Today, mental retardation is medically incurable; there is no medication that can cure it, no operation that can correct it.

It is difficult to understand this and live with it; it is natural for parents to take their child from doctor to doctor and often from quack to quack. The surge of hope with each visit and the inevitable disappointment only constitute unnecessary burdens on your souls. Besides, this is also an unnecessary drain on your pocketbook. There are parents who begin to hope anew every time they read about another medical discovery. This is understandable. But we must not forget that medication can be used only on a doctor's prescription and under a doctor's control. For instance, the currently fashionable indiscriminate use of vitamins is not as helpful as the layman might think; uncontrolled hormone treatments can also cause highly undesirable side effects.

It is not the worst parents who are ready to do "everything" for their infirm child; they often run the risk of trying unnecessary things, and what is worse, of expecting too much in the way of results. We know from experience that sooner or later all such parents realize that a "cure" is impossible. Mental retardation is really not a disease; it is a condition.

Yet there is help for your child! The therapy here is called "training." Of course, we must not hope to be able to cure mental retardation, but training can bring about a considerable improvement in behavior. We know from experience that there is a clear distinction between the well-trained and the untrained retarded child, even on the lowest level—even in the case of idiots.

You parents are the most important educators of your children, healthy or handicapped. In the case of the infirm child, your role is far more important. The foundations of training and education are laid at home, even in the case of the healthy child. In taking care of her child—in letting him share in her life—the mother is equipping the child to absorb the teaching of others. As soon as he can take his first steps, the healthy child will want to explore the world outside the home. Once outside, he will meet other children and other grownups who will influence his growth and development. In the case of the infirm child, there are no such other children and grownups who can contribute to his growth and development. The infirm child's contacts are confined to his parents.

This is why the way you handle the child is so important. You parents are the people who can do the most for your infirm child.

Therefore: don't look for miracle doctors or miracle drugs. You yourselves must do everything that can help improve your child's condition. When you realize that help cannot come from any other source, you will see that you can help your child much more than you might think. A fine and beautiful mission awaits you. You alone can accomplish it. The kind of life your handicapped child will lead depends on you. For this, you need no specialized training, no degree or diploma: your patience, your understanding, your love, your burning desire to help your child—these are far more important.

8

The Parents' Attitude

MARRIAGE is the soil on which children grow. No plant can thrive on poor soil. Your handicapped child is a very tender sprout: he needs an especially good soil if he is to grow. Work on your marriage, therefore! Your worries about your child must not separate you: they must become the strong bond that unites you. This child was given to both of you, together; and together you must care for him. Together, your misfortune is only half as hard to bear.

You should try to agree on all questions that concern the child; you will not get anywhere unless you pull together. You have a hard road ahead. You must walk hand in hand if you are to reach your destination.

Mother, please remember that the father of your child suffers just as much as you do. Fathers, too, can cry. It is the wife's noblest right to dry her husband's tears, for she is the only one to see them. Your husband may be a real man and a hard worker—he may even be "tough"—but when he has a handicapped child he needs a place where he can find consolation. Don't forget that you are not only the mother of your handicapped child, but also your man's wife.

Perhaps your husband is not as far along in accepting the child as you are. Men have a more objective outlook than women. You think the little one looks cute as he or she stands before you in his or her Sunday best. Your husband—despite the pretty clothes—notes that the child looks different from other children. He is far from being a bad father if he is not yet ready to let the men at the office see him with the child. Don't, therefore, insist that the child be taken along on the office picnic.

And, Father, remember that your wife has been wounded where it hurts the most. Motherhood is the very essence of a woman's life. In it a woman finds her greatest happiness, her truest fulfillment. Here, too, she feels her deepest grief, for here she is most vulnerable. When children thrive, a mother feels that her life has been a success. But when children fail, she feels that she has failed in life. Think, Father, of the heart of a woman who can never feel the most innocent kind of pride—a mother's pride.

Do not let your wife come to feel as though she were left alone with her hopeless child. Give your time to the little one; give as much of it as you can. Play with him; try to teach him something; take him for a walk; put him to bed now and then; but, above all, share in your wife's worry and sorrow about the child. You will be glad to discover that there are things that you can get your offspring to do that your wife cannot get it to accomplish. Not because she is going about it the wrong way, but because her chances of success are limited by the daily routine battle she must fight to teach the child the most necessary day-today functions. Your entrance on the scene always has the aura of something special—often almost festive. Help your wife now and then in taking care of the child, regardless of whether she is really overworked or whether you feel that she has enough time.

In helping take care of the child, you are doing much more than easing the physical burden on your wife. As she takes care of her child the mother is in communion with it. The two form a unit. If the father shows no interest in caring for the child and if he does not participate in his training, he will gradually be excluded from this community of mother and child—unintentionally, but inevitably. And this can lead to a gradual estrangement between spouses. Then the mother will almost seek refuge in the child: in the child she will seek and find her mission as well as food for her emotions. The parents will then have less and less in common; they will coexist; they will not be living together. And both will suffer as a result. For there is one immutable law of life: where one mate suffers, the other suffers. And where parents suffer, the child suffers. This, too, is certain.

Your attitude will have a decisive effect on the entire family; the mood of a home depends on the parents. They give peace and joy to a home. But you can only give what you have. This means that there must first be an inner peace within both of you. But this inner peace is not a gift. You must work hard for it. It is doubly important that the mother achieve her own peace of mind. As she wins her own inner peace she will be able to bestow peace on the entire family.

The opposite, unfortunately, is also true. If the mother

is maladjusted—if she cannot find inner peace, if she cannot accept her lot, if she rebels against her fate and if her morale is low—then the other members of the household will not find peaceful joy. The children will give vent to their uneasiness by being fidgety, by fighting and being obstinate, and by generally acting up. This is where the father comes in. This is where he can make his most important contribution to the training of his children. If he supports the mother—if he shelters her and gives her a feeling of security—she will not only do a far better job but she will also be happier doing it.

You must recognize and accept your child's real condition. Only then can you help him. Glossing over your child's condition, finding euphemisms for it in your own eyes and those of others, helps neither you nor your child. The only thing left to do is to see the child as he is—no matter how much he may differ from the image you had fashioned for yourselves. The child needs you to love him just as he is. You must be able to say, from the bottom of your hearts: "Yes, that is the way my child is; he is retarded—but I love him just the same." Only then can you help your child make progress.

Mentally retarded children are, first and foremost, children. Like other children, they need the warmth of the nest to thrive. They need to feel that their parents love them as they are: not because of their good features, but simply because they are an integral part of an indissoluble unit, a member of the family. The child's belief that the world is good, protective, and stimulating depends to a great extent on the parents' attitude; it depends on whether they look at life in a natural and kindly way—

whether they grant the child his right to exist and allow him to have his own life. We must accept these children as they are, but at the same time we must show them what they should be like. Of course, this is a contradiction. There is only one thing that can overcome this contradiction, and that is love. Only if we love the child as he is can we instill in him an obligation to try to be as he should be. Handicapped children are very sensitive in this respect.

A person who has had the good fortune to have parents who accept his limitations and at the same time further his capabilities will be far better equipped to handle difficulties and demands encountered in later life—despite his disability—than will the individual whose contact with his parents was somber darkness and gloom. In their role as the starting point of life, the parents remain the model —the image of the world—as their children see it. This is why the kind of parents you are and how you behave is so important.

You suffer much more from this mental retardation than your child. The child does not suffer as a result of his debility. The more he is handicapped, the less he is aware of it. Most retarded children have no idea that they are lacking in something. This should be a consolation for you. There is one kind of grief that is worse than your own grief, and that is the grief that comes with seeing the suffering of a beloved individual—especially your own child— without being able to help. You will not have this kind of sorrow with your mentally retarded child.

It is the dearest wish of all parents to see their children happy. In the case of healthy children, this goal is not always attainable because there are many life factors that parents are powerless to alter. Despite loving, wise, and good training and education, a normal child may be deeply unhappy for long periods during his lifetime. Not so the mentally retarded child. Loving parents can shield him from grief and give him those joys which he can appreciate. The retarded child who feels loved—whose existing capabilities are being developed, who is kept busy in an appropriate manner, of whom not too much is demanded—is a happy individual. In many of these children who grow up in a harmonious family, we get the impression that they are the happiest people on earth. It is up to you, parents, to see to it that your handicapped child develops into a happy individual.

9

Brothers and Sisters

WHAT ABOUT the other children? How will brothers and sisters feel toward the handicapped child?

This, again, depends to a very great extent on the attitude of the parents. If the parents treat the handicapped child in as natural a fashion as his condition permits, then his brothers and sisters will think much less about the situation than if the mother hovers over the handicapped child in constant tension and excitement. If the parents have really accepted the infirm child with all his limitations, the brothers and sisters are more likely to accept him.

Explain to your other children why and in what respect their little sister or brother is different. But a one-time explanation will not suffice. Do not expect your children to understand and accept that which you yourselves could not understand and accept right away. After the specialist explained the situation to you for the first time, you were not instantly capable of accepting your handicapped child's condition. Your healthy children cannot do this right away either. You must therefore be patient when they are irritated by certain peculiarities of their little sister or brother.

It is your normal children's lot to have a handicapped brother or sister. We would be doing them a disservice if we were to try to get them to live as though they did not have such a brother or sister. We cannot shield the healthy siblings from their fate: they must take this upon themselves, and they will grow and mature with it and through it. But we must give them time—sometimes perhaps more time than you parents need.

Do not expect your normal children to exhibit a degree of maturity for which they are too young. You cannot expect a four-year-old to understand why its six-year-old handicapped brother keeps knocking over its blocks. You cannot expect an eight-year-old mother of a doll to stand by silently while her handicapped little sister turns her doll household upside down. It is an important part of training to teach the mentally retarded child that he must not touch certain things. During this phase of training, the very understandable reactions of the normal siblings can be a big help.

But none of the children should come out on the short end. You parents must see to it that the handicapped child is not overly teased or pushed around by a more robust little brother, or that a smart little sister does not take advantage of his weakness, or that the infirm child is not shut out of all games. The other siblings will be more willing to let the handicapped child take part in their play if they know that the mother will see to it that they can from time to time play by themselves, without any constraints, without having to make room for the handicapped child.

On the other hand, neither must your healthy children be put at a disadvantage in any way. Don't give all of your time to the infirm child. Your normal children need you too; they need your time, your interest and concern. Your children must not get the impression that you exist only for the handicapped child. Otherwise they will begin to nurse a grudge against him which may stay with them for the rest of their lives, and this does not help the relationship between siblings. The infirm child is only one part of your family. He must learn to adjust to the family unit, just like the other children. This is an important part of his training, and we would be unfair if we were to try to spare him this part of his adjustment.

If the handicapped child has done something—if he has broken something or soiled himself or pulled young plants out of the ground—you must not punish the brother or sister for not doing a better job of watching the child; you must punish the child himself. A normal child will always take revenge on the person whose punishment he or she had to take. Of course we want the other siblings to feel responsible for the handicapped child. It is right and proper to strengthen this sense of responsibility. But even a normal child can accept only as much responsibility as he can handle in accordance with his own stage of development. Not every child feels praised and flattered when we call him or her a "big boy" or a "big girl." Not every child wants to be "big"—especially when "being big" only brings more duties and chores without any additional benefits. There are also normal children who want to remain "little." This, too, we must give them a chance to be—even if they do have a handicapped younger brother or sister.

The situation differs greatly, depending on whether the handicapped child is younger or older than his brothers and sisters. If the handicapped child is the youngest, the situation is much simpler. He remains the baby in the family, both for parents and siblings. The balance between siblings is then approximately normal: the littlest one is everyone's darling. If he is not spoiled or excessively favored by the parents, the situation can be relatively smooth.

But if the handicapped child is older, it will be considerably more difficult for the other siblings to develop the right relationship with him. The most difficult time comes when the normal child gradually "by-passes" the handicapped child—perhaps not so much in age and size as in skills, ability to think, and general mental maturity. There may then come a time when the normal child will be unable to understand why his bigger brother or sister cannot "really" be played with. The normal child may also object when more is demanded of him than of the handicapped brother or sister; this can especially be expressed in the distribution of "chores around the house." The normal child may also find it strange that he should sternly be forbidden to do things the handicapped child is only mildly reprimanded for, such as bed-wetting, neglect of table manners, crying, etc. In this situation, it is doubly important to refrain from spoiling the handicapped child. Nevertheless, it is unavoidable that we should ask and expect more of the normal child. The parents must compensate for this through love; that is to say, they must again and again show the normal child in word and tender deed how dear he, too, is to them.

When the normal children reach their awkward teens,

the mentally retarded child can be the parents' consolation. The growing normal child tends to move away from the parents: he gets out—into life. There is more or less open resistance to those who have been guiding his life for so long; the normal child will then become increasingly obstreperous at home. At this time many parents are glad to have at least one child who willingly adheres to family habits that have been implanted in him over the years; they are glad to have at least one "good" child. The mentally retarded child is gladdened by the old family customs or by the mother's singing in the evening— even during those years when the other growing siblings more or less definitely reject these and other manifestations of family tradition. We know from experience that children can gradually move away from their parents—as they must—in a much more peaceful manner when the parents do not excessively hold on to their growing children, because they have a handicapped child who needs their care and attention and rewards them with childlike loyalty.

On the other hand, the growing up of normal children can bring a time of crisis for all siblings, especially when the infirm child is still far behind in his assimilation of the rules of human unity. There may be a feeling of rejection, even if all siblings got along well in the past. This is connected with the general ferment in the nature of teen-agers. Vanity is often excessive then, and the normal child will be ashamed of his retarded brother or sister. A high school student may be really angry at his mother when she picks him up in front of the school, with his abnormal little brother sitting in the front seat of the car. And the teen-age girl may object to wearing the sweater her mother knitted of the same wool used for her retarded baby sister's. "Does everybody have to know right off that we're sisters?" The growing normal teen-ager may not want the retarded brother or sister to be present when a favorite beau comes calling or when she is having a party.

All this does not point to a conclusive, unwelcome development in the relationship between siblings. Here, too— as in so many other situations—parents must be tactful if they have teen-agers in the house. In the long run, it will do the younger child no good if his presence is constantly forced on the older ones. It will help all the children in their relations with each other if the retarded child is tactfully kept in the background on certain occasions—without making the child feel badly. As soon as the teen-ager develops his or her own judgment, all these unpleasant things will pass. Parents will then find it beautiful to watch their maturing children lovingly assume responsibility for a retarded brother or sister. In well-adjusted families, this is not the exception; happily, it is the rule.

10

Relatives and Neighbors

IT IS NOT ONLY parents and siblings who must live with the
retarded child, but also relatives, friends, acquaintances,
and neighbors. Therefore, every mother who has brought
an obviously retarded child into the world tortures herself
with the questions: What will the rest of the family say?
How am I going to face them?

As long as parents are still uncertain in their attitude
toward a child, they cannot easily talk about it with other
people. As long as you cannot accept your child's limitations—you feel—so long can others not be expected to understand your problems. If you keep embellishing your
child's condition, you are in effect trying to erect an edifice
of secrets and euphemisms, even lies, for whose continua-
tion you are going to expend much useless energy. You feel
that this edifice is threatened even if someone merely asks
how the child is getting along; you suspect some sort of
hidden probe behind this inquiry. And if someone—generally without any ulterior motive—happens to ask how

old the child is, you are deeply hurt. And so you prefer to withdraw from people.

This is not good for you; it hurts the entire family, especially your retarded child. You are in effect inhibiting him in his contact with other people; you are preventing him from learning, in a natural way, how to deal with other people. Every child needs this kind of contact if he is to develop.

As long as you refuse to admit that there is something lacking in your child, you will be trying to embellish his condition in the eyes of others. This does not help. The others probably noticed, even *before* you did, that your child is not like other children. People have a habit of looking at other people's children in a much more objective manner than at their own; they notice faults and shortcomings in other children much sooner than in their own.

We know from experience that retarded children who are well trained and well behaved can have very lovable personalities. Anyone meeting such a child will soon shed any prejudices he or she may have had. It may be necessary for you to discuss your child's condition openly with a neighbor; you may have to talk to him or her about your child's limitations and your sorrow. And your neighbor will then talk to his children in order to enable them to understand your child and give him help or protection.

This applies to your relatives, too. Here, again, the parents' calm and objective attitude will be a big help. You can discourage excessive protestations of sympathy if you yourselves realize that this child—like any other child—will bring you joy as well as trouble. Once your relatives see that you have a positive attitude toward your child, they will feel less obligated to give unsolicited advice; this will help you prevent much in the way of uncertainty, tension, and disagreement. Persistent advice from neighbors and acquaintances, urging you to try this or that medication, this or that quack, will no longer rob you of the painfully acquired attitude of accepting the unalterable.

On the other hand, relatives who really love the child can be a great help to you and to the child by now and then taking care of him and giving you a respite.

Do not be reluctant to accept such help. It will not be good for your marriage if, year after year, you never go out together because one of you—generally the mother— must always stay with the child day and night. Do not underestimate your relatives' or neighbors' willingness and ability to help.

It will also be good for your child if now and then he can spend some time with people other than the two of you. He will learn how to get along with others. This is an absolutely necessary preparation for later life. When relatives or acquaintances offer to take your child along with them for an afternoon, a day, or maybe even several days, be grateful and accept. This will be good preparation for the day when you may have to send your child away, perhaps because he must go to the hospital or because Mother is sick or for some other reason. This is also good preparation for the day when the child will have to start going to school. "Sending him or her away" should never be made to look like punishment; it should always be made to appear as a reward and as a joyous event.

Children who are always with their mothers are afraid of people whom they do not know, even if the person happens to be an uncle or godmother. The "stranger" must not overwhelm the child with tenderness; that will only frighten him. It is better to seem to ignore the child for awhile, to give him a chance to observe the "newcomer," and only then to try to win his confidence with kindness or candy.

Other children—for instance, most of the Mongoloids —are quite open in showing their liking for other people. They hug everybody and are generous with their kisses. This may be repulsive to most people, even though they may try hard not to show it in front of the parents. The retarded child must therefore be taught from the very beginning that he may touch only his parents and siblings.

Retarded children, like all other children, are capable of loving. They may even be much more willing to give love. We "normal" people often find that we simply "cannot stand" this or that person, even though he or she may like us. Not so with mentally retarded children. They love him who loves them. It is often marvelous to see how sensitively these children react to the love offered them. They love those who give them of their time, who care for them, who are kind to them. They are happy when they can show their affection.

It is up to you parents to teach these children how they can best show their love, perhaps with a friendly smile, some little service, or a gift. This is much better than teaching the child to express his affection only through hugging and kissing. This can become a habit that may make trouble for you later as the child gets older.

We know that small children like to play alone up to a certain age: they are not yet interested in other children.

The situation here is the same with the retarded infant, and it continues much longer than in the case of the normal child. Even at an age when other children play together happily and peacefully, the social development of the retarded child may still be in the phase in which he does not know what to do with playmates. Don't force him to play with other children; above all, don't force other children to play with him. Gradually try to bring other children into his environment. It may be that both normal and retarded child, when brought together, will continue to play alone, without paying much attention to each other. Still, the retarded only child will get the impression that there are other little human beings in the world. It may be that he will be able to play with others only after we have taught him some of the simplest group games.

The mentally retarded child must not be allowed to play in the street without supervision as we might let normal children play under these conditions. This would be beyond the child's capabilities. He may run into unforeseen or unaccustomed situations with which he cannot cope or react to properly. And he does not know how far from home he can go.

Besides, on the street he may meet children who do not know him and who are not used to his looks and peculiarities. The other children may laugh at him or—what is worse—lead him into mischief. If this should happen, it usually does little good to scold the other children. This only makes things worse, because they will then vent their anger on the retarded child; they will feel that the latter was responsible for their being reprimanded. The only thing for the mother to do is to stay nearby and keep an eye on the children, at least until they can play together without any untoward incidents. While keeping an eye on them in this manner, she should try to do some suitable chore. Unobtrusive observation may be necessary for years. Whether we can let our retarded child play with the rest of the children in the neighborhood depends not so much on them as on the peculiar character of our own child. Every unwelcome incident must show us where and in what respect we must still teach our child to get along with others.

A well-behaved child is much more likely to be accepted by his environment than an ill-mannered one. This also applies to retarded children. If your child learns the basic rules of human conduct, he will be loved by both relatives and acquaintances.

11

It Is You Who Must Teach Your Child

IN THE CASE of a normal child, it is natural for parents to guide and foster his development in such a manner that he will become a useful member of society and manage to be as happy as possible in this role. It is just as natural to help the retarded child to approach this goal as closely as his condition permits. If we get the retarded child to a point where he is happy, peaceable, well behaved, clean, and obedient, people will treat him in a much friendlier fashion. He will then also be much more manageable at home and the entire family will have a more peaceful and happier life.

A well-behaved child gets many more expressions of sympathy than an ill-mannered one. The friendliness with which he is treated, again, has a salutary effect on his character: he will come to feel that he is loved. Like all other people, the retarded child will derive satisfaction from this. And thus he will develop into a satisfied human being and will repay kindness with kindness. He will feel accepted, and he will in turn accept the demands of the situation. He will fit into his expanding world in an increasingly harmonious fashion.

But the ill-mannered child offends everyone. He is corrected again and again, not only by people close to him, but by others with whom he has no emotional ties. He will then meet much hostility and react with a hostility of his own; and this will only make him more unpopular. Small wonder that, under these circumstances, he perceives the world as a hostile place; he is, after all, locked in constant battle with this world. He lives, so to speak, in enemy territory. Instead of harmonious adjustment, he develops a spirit of quarrelsomeness: he resists everything, struggles against everybody, and moreover, uses the kind of methods that cause his environment to reject him even more. Thus we get the picture of an intractable, aggressive retarded child who smashes everything, makes trouble for everybody, and is a burden to all. Aggressiveness is not a part of the clinical picture of mental retardation; it is a result of the wrong kind of treatment.

The normal child is also stubborn for a time. On occasion he is unmanageable as the result of a particular situation, but if we talk to him calmly, the child will develop understanding and self-control and adopt the right kind of behavior. The mentally deficient child fights with much poorer—though all the more intensive—means. He is far more subject to his emotions, because reason is lacking.

This is why we must make sure that he does not become set in a defensive, rejecting type of behavior that will be-

come a habit. The best preventive here is our own attitude.
Our love, our calm friendliness, will evoke friendly and
peaceable behavior in the retarded child. If, in addition,
we teach him the forms of proper behavior, other people
will treat him in a friendly manner. And thus the child
will have no occasion for aggressive attitudes.

The retarded child must be taught much that the normal
child learns by himself as soon as he has reached a certain
age. Many of the things the normal child simply picks up
as he goes along, the retarded child must learn. One fine
day the normal child simply has acquired another new
skill: he can put on or take off his socks, or he drinks out
of a cup—all this without our having to spend time teaching him.

In the case of the retarded child, this does not come as
easily. By himself, he learns little or nothing. But if you
take the time and the trouble, you will be amazed how
much you can teach him to do. During the first five or
six years, you are your child's only guides. Use this time
well; it will bear fruit.

12

Good Habits

IN A RETARDED CHILD, training is largely habituation. For all of us, good habits constitute the most important factor in everyday life and in our contacts with others—even if we may not give much thought to this. How much more does this apply to the retarded! For the latter, good habits can and must mean the difference between "good" and "bad." A normally endowed person is rudderless if he or she is not guided by moral principles; a retarded person is rudderless when he or she is not guided by good habits. The retarded individual cannot make his or her own judgments; he will act according to the habits we have instilled in him.

You must therefore get the child accustomed to a regular daily routine from the very beginning; let him feel the rhythm of the day. Once he has become used to the fact that one activity follows another, he will be more ready and willing to cooperate. He will come to know that he has to get up in the morning. Then comes the trip to the

bathroom. Then washing and dressing. After that, breakfast, and so on.

The sequence of these and other daily recurring functions must be maintained. This will make your child feel
secure. Retarded children are conservative and against any
sudden changes in routine. It will confuse the child if you
suddenly serve him breakfast without first giving him a
chance to wash his face; he will probably react in a cranky
fashion.

You must, therefore, from the very beginning, teach the
child *only those habits that he can retain.* This will save
you laborious retraining later on. Once you have accustomed your child to sitting on his toilet seat in the living
room, he will object strenuously if you suddenly—"just for
now"—move the whole setup to the bathroom because
you are having a visitor. Or: if your child is used to licking
the plate, he will also do so when you are visiting somewhere, no matter how embarrassed you may be.

You will want your retarded child to greet people in the
customary fashion, the way other children do. Don't,
therefore, get him used to a form of greeting which he will
later have to *unlearn* laboriously, such as throwing kisses
or simply waving. It will be easier for you and better for
your child if he learns the proper form of greeting from the
start—that is to say, if he is taught to shake hands. Later
on, when he can talk, you can teach him to say "How do
you do?" and "Good-bye." If you teach him to say "Hi!"
and "Bye-bye," you will find it embarrassing later when
he greets persons entitled to a formal greeting in this
manner simply because he cannot judge when the formal

greeting is in order and when the informal greeting is called for.

Teach your retarded child the same forms of courtesy you are trying to teach your normal children, such as saying "Thank you," asking for things, being silent when adults are talking, waiting his turn, etc. Get him used to everyday life. Get him accustomed to trying to respond to a question with an answer. See that he learns to respond to a request as best he can; in other words, you must teach him obedience. Train him so that he will make his wishes known in suitable form. Let him see that acting up will get him nowhere and that a polite request is the only way to your heart—the only way that opens closed doors, be it your front door or the door to the cabinet where you keep the candy.

It takes your normal children many years to learn the forms of civilized conduct; every mother must keep saying the same thing over and over again, year after year. But no mother should ever give up trying to remind her children of proper manners. Do not give up trying to do the same for your retarded child. The best thing you can do for him is to get him used to acting like a well-behaved, polite, and friendly person. This is the only way he can win the sympathy of others.

Only habit can keep a retarded child aware of what he may and what he may not do. You may tell him not to go here or there, not to leave the garden, never to do this or that again—but all these commands have only momentary meaning. The retarded child violates a prohibition, not because he is disobedient, but because he is simply no longer aware or not yet aware that he must not do this or that. It is therefore useless to make your punishment more severe each time as with normal children; calm constancy of discipline is much better.

For instance, if we want the child to get the idea that he is to stay in the garden, we must not wait until he has slipped out and then look for him and punish him severely after we have found him. This does not help. We will be astonished to find that he will run away again, the first chance he gets. After all, there is so much to be seen out on the street, and the departure from the garden is so far back in his consciousness that he does not connect this act with the subsequent punishment. It is better if we keep watching and take action just as the child starts opening the garden gate. In the well-trained child, this creates a barrier which he will not ignore and which is more effective than any wire fence.

Of course this kind of training takes time; but it is worth the trouble. This is the only way we can keep the re-tarded child from offending others within or outside the family. It is better to develop a certain good habit in the child in a calm and constant manner than to reprimand him after he has done something wrong.

We must not chuckle when the little rascal does some-thing naughty. If he does the same thing ten years later, no one will find it cute; people will find him an unbearable brat. Don't delay in changing his naughty actions until they have become offensive to everyone and take root in the form of bad habits.

You must see to it that your child does not acquire any bad mannerisms. Make sure that he does not pick up the habit of weaving forward and back with the upper part of the body or of uninterruptedly making the same hand movements. If he should monotonously keep rolling a small piece of paper between his fingers, put something else into his hand, to arouse his interest. It is also a good idea to see that he does not handle his toys in exactly the same way all the time, such as doing nothing but turning the wheel when playing with his toy car or knocking two blocks together in the same manner. This sort of thing does not constitute play and does not help the child make progress. Do not let him sit around for hours, doing such monotonous things, even if he may seem quite satisfied. Try not only to divert his attention but also to get him to take an interest in a better form of play.

But you must also stop the child when he restlessly runs from one room to the next, without reason and without looking at anything. Try to divert his attention to a sedentary activity, at least for a short time.

Definitely restrain the child when he sticks his hand down his throat to make himself throw up; when he starts pulling on his eyes, ears, or other parts of the body that are better left alone; when he puts things in his mouth that are not for eating. A mother can make a very small child understand when she does not want him to do something and can make it clear to the child that he must stop.

Monotonous habits take root in the child, especially at a time when he is not yet interested in the outside world. If you don't want your child to have bad habits, you must try to direct his attention to something else. Once a bad habit has been acquired, it is far more difficult to correct it in a retarded child than in another child who has many other interests.

Normal children—and adults—often have two sets of behavior: one for at home, and the other for the rest of the world. The retarded individual has but one set of behavior. Be sure it is a good set.

In the case of retarded children, the environment in which they grow up is far more important than in the case of normal children. The latter can distinguish between good and bad; the former cannot. They simply copy what they see and hear and they copy indiscriminately. If a retarded child is generally spoken to in a loving and polite manner at home, he will adopt a polite tone. But if he is snapped and shouted at, we must not be surprised when he tends to be gruff.

There are parents who adopt a tone toward their children which they would not dare use toward anyone else. Of course, the retarded child does try your patience sorely; it is natural for it to wear thin now and then. But don't forget that you are your child's model, even when you lose your temper; try to contain yourselves. If in anger you call your child a name, do not be surprised when he addresses you or other people by the same name. Then you will find that it is much harder to break a bad habit than to teach a good one.

13

How Am I Going to Teach Him Anything?

HERE are some helpful rules:

1. *Treat your retarded child as much as possible as you would a normal child.* But do not expect the retarded child to react the way the normal child would. Do not expect the impossible, but do not give up. Be grateful for the smallest amount of progress; it shows that further advance is possible.

2. *Retarded children learn only that which they repeat often.* Your child must repeat minor or even very minor functions many times until he gets them right. This means that you will have to practice many things with him each day. A little each day is better than long practice sessions now and then. When a child tires, his attention flags.

3. *Give the child enough time.* Do not keep driving and hounding him. Retarded children often move very slowly. We must let them move at the speed dictated by their life rhythm. You can step up the tempo only very

gradually. As soon as a certain activity or function has ceased to be difficult for the child, he will perform it faster.

4. *On the other hand, do not allow him to "dawdle" when he is supposed to do something.* It is difficult for the child to focus on a certain goal. You must help him remember his particular chore of the moment. Even the healthy child goes through a development stage in which he handles everything he encounters. He is so completely absorbed in his handling of things that he does not care what happens to the things he handles. This kind of activity is not useless, even though not aimed at a particular objective. By handling things, the child learns about them in their environment and gets to know various materials and substances; he discovers what can be made out of these things. The normal child will progress beyond this stage very soon and will devise his own play goals. Not so the retarded child. He stays in the stage of nonspecific handling of things much longer, and there are some retarded children who never outgrow this stage. This is why it is all the more important for us to give the retarded child goals—small goals.

5. *See that the child finishes what he has started.* Nothing should be left half done. The task you give the child should be small enough so that its completion will not be beyond the child's abilities. The child must find out for himself what "finished" means. In time, he will acquire the habit of finishing what he has started.

6. *Show the child how to do things.* This is much better than merely telling him how to do them. The best method is for you to perform the particular task along with the

child; that is, you will guide his hands until he can perform the particular function by himself. In this manner you will prevent the child from learning the wrong way of doing things.

7. *Help the child only when it is really necessary.* Let the child do everything he can or wants to do by himself. Of course, everything goes much faster when you are doing it (and you will be doing a better job of it, too), but your child will not be learning anything; he will grow too dependent on you. If your child wants to do something by himself, don't say, "Oh, you can't do that." The child might just believe you and never try to do the particular thing again. Don't take anything out of the child's hands once he has begun trying to do something, no matter how clumsily he may start. The very fact that he is trying to do something by himself shows that he is ready to learn the particular function. If you help your child all the time, he will become spoiled and will find it difficult to tackle more involved activities. Then you will have a little magician on your hands who gets others to do everything for him with the simple words: "Draw me a horse!" or "Make me a toy!"

8. *Your child can only learn the things for which he has the right degree of maturity.* You must refrain from aiming at goals that are beyond the child's abilities. You can only introduce him to those things he can absorb and assimilate in accordance with his degree of maturity at the particular moment. You must make success possible for the child by keeping his tasks within his range of maturity and capabilities. Don't despair if the child simply cannot learn a certain thing; perhaps it is too soon for him to learn how to

handle a certain object. Put it aside. Try it again after some time has passed; it will go better, you will find.

9. *Do not demand too much of your child.* If you expect him to do things he is incapable of, he will surely fail. Even the mentally retarded child knows when he has failed; he can sense when he does not come up to his parents' expectations. If this happens frequently, the child will become so anxious that he will not dare tackle anything any more. He will retreat and sink deeper into dependence or even passivity, but deep inside he may also rebel against excessive demands. He will then become stubborn, rejecting, and difficult to manage.

10. *Teach your child only one thing at a time.* As soon as he has mastered one motion well enough so that he no longer needs to think while performing it, you can go on to the next little motion or step. The various steps in learning how to do things will probably have to be much smaller than you imagined. This is why you must break every task down into its component parts and practice these parts until the child has really mastered them. Only then can you go on. For instance, it is useless for you to insist that the child not spill soup as he scoops it out of a bowl with a spoon while completely absorbed in the task of just finding his mouth with the spoon.

11. *Be sure your instructions are clear and understandable;* that your child has really understood you. Always use the same words for the same functions or actions. Long explanations as to purpose and goal are useless; they only confuse the retarded child. Besides, your child probably will not understand long speeches. He may listen attentively in the beginning, but he will soon give up, because

he does not understand after all, no matter how much he may want to. If this should happen often, there is a danger that the child will come to accept your long-winded explanations and exhortations simply as a kind of natural noise to which he will no longer pay any attention. It is better to give short, easily understood instructions and brief admonitions.

12. *Show your satisfaction when the child has done something correctly.* The retarded child needs more praise than another child, because he is easily fatigued. He has little interest in things, and his desire to discover—to try things—is at best rather weak. The child is thus not motivated to perform purposeful acts. Your praise must reinforce his perseverance, must give him the desire for renewed effort and confidence, and new hope that he can master a particular task. If you are proud of what your child can do, he, too, will be proud of his accomplishment and will have the desire to repeat his performance or perhaps even do better next time.

13. If you and your child are engaged in some kind of joint activity, *the situation must never have the appearance of an examination.* The child must not get the idea that you can hardly wait for him to solve or fail to solve a particular problem. While you are giving simple instructions, you must in no way express any doubt as to the possibility of success. On the contrary, be very definite in showing your satisfaction with what the child has accomplished.

14. *Do not scold the child if he has done something incorrectly.* This failure is mostly due to inability rather than to unwillingness. Of course, criticism is necessary, but to reprove a child who is doing his best is certainly improper.

We must expect little "accidents on the job." We can avoid them only if we want to prevent any activity on the child's part—and this is not our intention. In setting the table, the child may drop a plate; he may stain his clothes while feeding himself. These and other "accidents" are the tuition we and our child must pay on the way to independent activity. If a child has done some damage without intending to, we must calm him. "You really tried hard; let's hope you'll make out better next time." Unthinking scolding or a thoughtless slap in the face could result in the child's never trying the same activity again because of fear of what would happen to him if he should have another mishap.

15. *Don't forget the value of the good example.* Many children have a tendency to imitate whatever they see going on in their environment. The way you eat, the way you talk to each other, the way you behave—all these serve as examples for the child in his own behavior. You must see to it that your behavior is such that you will be pleased to see it mirrored in your child's actions.

14

When Should I Teach My Child?

THERE IS *much* you will be able to teach your child in the course of the day—just as it happens to occur. Throughout the day, you will be able to show your child, over and over again, how he can meet the requirements of particular situations. This is the way normal children learn—the only difference is that we never think of it that way. The normal child learns how to do the hundreds of little daily chores and functions by watching the mother or getting instructions from her. He observes the mother, is increasingly interested in her activities, crawls after her while she is doing her housework, imitates her, and in this manner learns all he needs to know at his age. He also watches the mother wash her face, take a bath, get dressed, and so on. The normal child's healthy drive soon causes him to perform these activities himself. The healthy baby and small child "learn" a tremendous amount long before they go to school and even if they are not specifically taught. As a matter of fact, the normal child learns more during the first three years of his life than during the first three years of school. In the beginning of his existence on earth, life itself is his teacher; his incentive is a desire to know and to do things.

The situation is not as simple in the case of the retarded child; by himself, he learns little or almost nothing. He lacks the incentive of the normal child. He has less desire to know and to do; these desires may be entirely absent during the first years of life. This is why you will have to teach the retarded child from the very beginning. And in this respect you are not alone.

The mother of a normal baby also teaches her child many useful things—when she hands him a rattle or talks to him or picks up a toy for him. These may seem like small details, but they are important in the child's development. We know that children who are not cared for properly—whom no one talks to, who are left alone for many hours during the day, for whom no one ever picks up a toy they have dropped—are, at the end of the first year, behind those children who were lovingly and conscientiously cared for by their mothers. The fact that such children are behind in their development also is expressed in their awkwardness in handling various objects; after all, they have had much less opportunity to handle things than their lovingly cared-for contemporaries.

Lack of opportunity to be active and do things can, however, result not only from insufficient care, but also from excessive care. There are overanxious mothers who—out of fear that their child might suffer harm—refrain from letting the child handle all kinds of toys. There are mothers who—out of an exaggerated sense of neatness—do not allow the child to play with something that is not a toy, even though almost any object can become a desirable toy for a small child. The great differences encountered here are illustrated by a comparison of two two-year-old children; one of them (the normal one) handled 71 different objects during the day, while the retarded child handled only 14. The normal child thus had a far greater radius of activity and potential for learning than the retarded child, and this of course also influences the progress of mental development.

Don't let your baby lie in his crib, ignored from morning till night, even if he does act satisfied and demands nothing. It is entirely possible that your child may have to stay in the playpen for a long time; try to make this small area a lively one, even if the child never asks for a change in routine.

Every normal mother reacts to a normal baby in a normal fashion. The reaction here is a reciprocal one. The two stimulate each other. The healthy infant summons the mother long before he can talk, and makes her understand that he wants something. The baby's needs arouse the mother's instinctive drive to satisfy these needs. The child reacts in his own particular fashion, and this again causes the mother to engage in further activity with the child. The little one may sound off when he has dropped his rattle; the mother will then stand by the cot, talk to the baby, and put the toy back in his hand.

Now, if the child's reaction is not forthcoming (as in the case of the retarded child), the mother will offer him less in the way of stimulation, without even being aware of this. She will talk less to him and she will hand him toys more rarely, because the child, after all, does not do anything with them. Thus the child will have less opportunity to gather experience even at this early age.

In the case of the retarded child, it is particularly necessary to offer him systematically those opportunities for activity which he cannot create for himself spontaneously.

If the baby does not yet reach for things, start with some kind of toy that will cause him to focus his attention. You might hang a multicolored ball or a balloon or a colored pennant or a bunch of colored paper strips over the crib—any object that will move with the slightest breeze. You might use chains of colored glass balls suspended from a ring and giving off a wonderfully soft sound when stirred by a gentle breeze. However, these and other toys should not hang over the crib at all times, but only at certain hours. Try to get your child to focus his attention on them.

If it appears that your child notices too few things, encourage him to look around. Take him to the window often and point out the moving cars in the street. If that does not interest him, perhaps you will have more success with a colored flashlight or with a small mirror with which you can make the sunlight dance.

Try to get your child to focus attention on you; talk to him, sing to him, and try to get him to look at you. Persevere in your efforts to get him to smile. This often takes patience.

Looking around is an important activity. Give your child plenty of opportunity to look around. The healthy infant will soon try to peek out into the world. The retarded child is not as curious. This is why it is best to keep him in a crib from where he can see things even before he can sit up.

But the retarded child should not spend his days in the crib for too long a period of time, even if he does not try to stand up. He will make better progress if you put him in a walker. He gets much better support from the walker and from the hard floor, especially if you help him along.

Using the walker is a big step forward; it gives the child a chance to see more. Of course, here, too, there is a danger that, once strapped in, he might do nothing. There is a tendency to leave him there because he seems quite happy.

The child's first important activity is grasping. The first toy the child gets is usually a rattle. This gives him a chance to practice grasping. Some children make rather awkward movements with a rattle and often treat their faces in an ungentle manner; the mother is then reluctant to put anything into the child's hand, for fear he might hurt himself. This fear is unfounded: no child has ever hurt himself with a rattle. Even a normal baby will now and then bang himself on the nose with it. But after some practice, he will find out which kind of movements he had better avoid.

There are retarded children who do not grip a rattle because they shy away from the cold, hard feel of the celluloid or plastic. But you can get them to grasp things if you hand them soft objects such as a woollen ball or a piece of cloth (perhaps rolled up to form a stick). Every type of material requires a different grip. It is helpful to have the child practice the various types of grips by handing him different kinds of material. You can give him stick-shaped objects of varying weight and consistency, thinner or thicker objects, lighter or heavier articles, wooden objects, metal rods, rubber hoses, etc. You can also sew wide and narrow strips of silk, wool, velvet, etc., onto a large, strong ring that cannot be opened. This will cause the child to try to grasp and pluck. Naturally you will have to keep replacing these items as they become soiled and worn. Plastic objects are certainly more hygienic, but we cannot confine ourselves to them exclusively in the case of the retarded child. This is why: if the child does not really try to reach for anything, it may often be because the material we are handing him does not look inviting.

Generally these children like woolen or silken-plush animals. These are the toys our normal children sometimes treasure up to school age and beyond. The normal child never loves a plastic or shiny cloth animal as much. You will rarely see a retarded child still playing with the same old soft fuzzy animal after a long period of time. Such toys are harder to keep clean, especially when the child drools. But they are more stimulating when it comes to touch and handling.

Large, light-weight chains such as those for normal infants are also good for our children. The chain should consist of balls made up of wood, or rubber, plastic, cork, wool, etc. These objects must not be strung too closely; they must be movable. The child then learns to move the objects back and forth, to turn and twist them, and to hit the chain with his hand in order to make them dangle.

Rubber animals are also good for gripping practice. The child finds out that every action brings a reaction, a certain effect: the animal squeaks when squeezed.

If you notice that your baby is using his hands too infrequently, you must keep encouraging him to play with them often in ever-new ways. Teach him to "patty-cake," to wave "bye-bye" and so on.

You will offer your child all these and many other things in the course of the day. The best thing to do is to stand by the crib or playpen several times a day, for ten to fifteen minutes, and play with the child whenever you can spare the time, especially when the little one is in a good mood.

But there comes a time when this is not enough, when your child will need more in the way of training. From that time on, you should sit down at a table with the child and "work" with him each day. You should try to teach him the things he should gradually be learning—the things you feel he might be able to learn now. This should be a regularly scheduled "working time." Your child will thus develop the good habit of concentrating on purposeful activity for a certain period of time—and you will find it easier to get him to do that. At any rate, this period should come only when the little one is well rested, fresh, and in a good mood. The time after the afternoon nap is good. You should pick a time when your other children are in school or can keep busy by themselves. You and your retarded child must then be undisturbed.

Just how long this "work period" is supposed to take depends entirely on your child's condition. At first, you might try to keep the child occupied with purposeful activity for half an hour. This does not mean that he must keep doing the same thing during this entire period. He will hardly be capable of doing this in the beginning. In the beginning, his interest—in anything at all—will only be rather fleeting. You must get the child to concentrate more and more on the same thing. Increase this period gradually, watch in hand. Your patience is not a reliable yardstick of time. Don't keep the child doing the same thing until your patience gives out; this can happen either too soon or too late. Don't stop when both of you simply cannot stand it any more; stop when you intended to stop.

The second part of this book contains a list of some things the retarded child should and can learn. On the basis of this list, you can prepare a work program. You will perhaps think of additional things you may want to teach the child. Not all retarded children develop in the same manner. Your child may be able to do some things entirely by himself, without your having to practice these things with him. Perhaps a certain activity that you want to teach the child and that seems easy to you will prove too difficult for him. It will be better to postpone teaching that particular skill until later.

The less endurance your child has, the more often will you have to change his activity. Don't keep him occupied with the same activity for too long; on the other hand, stop only after a certain phase in learning has been completed. Then your child will experience the satisfaction of having completed something, and completing a task will become a habit.

Always start with the activity your child likes. For instance, with a song or a game involving the fingers, or a short rhyme. Then take up a quiet activity—that is, an activity during which the child must sit still. After that, give the child something to do which will allow him to move or walk around; then again follow up with a sedentary task. You can finish up with something the child likes to do, so that he will come away from this working time with good memories.

The working time should be a joyous event. Just as normal children are happy when the mother sits down with them and participates in their games, so your retarded child should be glad when you belong to him exclusively for a certain period of time. This is why this period should be filled with calm, peaceful activity.

Scolding and coercion do not promote success. On the contrary, they frighten the child away from further activity. Scolding and coercion cause the child to become excited and perhaps even stubborn.

15

What Should the Child Learn?

WE CANNOT LIST all the things a child should and can learn. Like the normal child, the retarded child must learn to use his physical and other abilities. He must learn to do chores and do them as well as he can. He must learn to take on responsibility to the degree to which he can be expected to do so. He must learn perseverance and concentration and many, many other things. If you train your child carefully and lovingly, he will acquire all these skills to the degree permitted by his condition.

We can bring up our children only with the help of the specific tasks they encounter in their existence as children. Good training must and will be expressed in the child's actions. If the child is treated correctly, his training will always result in better performance, and this improvement in its turn serves to develop the child's personality. In this manner we also can develop stunted faculties in the case of the retarded child; this at the same time serves to develop his character.

The specific task of parents of retarded children is to

get their child to a point where he can take care of his daily needs by himself. He will thus cease to be dependent on others in every single situation. This is not only a relief for the parents but also constitutes a calming factor as regards the future. In addition, experience has shown that the child needs a certain degree of self-reliance in order to be happy. Retarded children are much happier, much easier to manage and educate, when they can take care of themselves, when they can do little chores for others, and keep busy by themselves.

However, these children lack the wealth of experience that comes with exploring their environment; they lack the practice in the use of their capacities that the normal child gets daily and hourly. The playlike discovery, exploration, and practice that the normal child gets are very valuable because of their large variations and variety and their great degree of irregularity; the latter precludes any possibility of fatigue. These discoveries and exercises are so numerous and constitute such excellent training from the very first day onward, that not even the best child-guidance expert could devise a better system. The mentally retarded child is denied this natural form of schooling. His drive is weak, his energy feeble. Retarded children remain on the same level of development far too long unless they are stimulated from the outside. This danger exists not only in those children who sit around inactively, but also in children who are constantly moving around, whose motor unrest does not give them a chance for quiet observation and sensible activity.

This is why *daily practice*—systematic daily practice—is needed.

16

General Training

THE RETARDED CHILD must in time be taught how to keep pursuing a certain goal, if we want to make sure that he will engage in meaningful activity later on. Even the retarded child can become accustomed to meaningful activity with the help of suitable toys or games. This is why we must not give him any toy just to keep him quiet. Retarded children are easily satisfied, but the satisfied handling of just any object must not be our most important objective. Otherwise it may happen that at the age of twenty years our child will do nothing but fondle things contentedly; that sight, no mother or father can stand. This is why, from the very beginning, the toy must be shaped so that it will stimulate the child and cause him to engage in purposeful activity. Parents must actively participate in the play activities of the retarded baby and must be aware of the educational value of these activities.

We have mentioned the important function of grasping. If the child can grasp, he should also learn how to let go. At first, a child lets go of an object because he loses interest in it. Now we must teach him to let go deliberately. This is why we give him toys he can push or roll—a ball or a toy car or an animal mounted on wheels. Now we want the little one to push or roll the toy toward us; we catch the toy and roll it back toward the child. This helps us hold the child's attention for a longer period of time.

The child can now connect two things, move them together, or knock them together. We show him how we can take a block or stick and knock on the table with the object. We put a block in each of the child's hands and let him knock them together, first slowly, then faster and faster. Most children like the noise they are making in this manner. For many a retarded child, intentional noisemaking becomes a frequent game. This desire to make noise can be made useful. We teach the child to hit a small suspended bell with a stick, or a drum with a drumstick, and he is simultaneously getting a form of target practice.

Another way of bringing objects together is the filling and emptying of containers, as well as the stacking of boxes, one within the other. Boxes of varying size arouse the child's interest, even the greatly retarded one. Now he wants cube pyramids, consisting of hollow wooden cubes, the smaller ones of which can always easily be inserted into the larger ones. This toy has many uses. The child can move them around, push them, and make a noise with them. We teach the child to slide one hollow cube into the next, to line them up next to each other, or to stack them on the table in the form of a tower; to place larger cubes over smaller ones, etc. Of course the child will not be doing all this from the very beginning; in most cases, he will be happy when we practice these things with him.

Based on the same principle, we also have sets of balls, barrels, rings, and the like, made of plastic; these sets can also be inserted into each other, but the difficulty lies in the fact that these containers must be closed before we can go on to the next step. We do not encounter this difficulty in the case of hollow cubes. The shapes that can be closed give us a chance to practice the closing of boxes with the child.

Once the child can insert things into each other, we can give him a stick that is firmly inserted in a base plate; such items are available in wood or plastic at most toy stores. Now we can practice the stacking of rings on the stick. In the beginning, the sequence does not matter. Later we let the child know that the rings are of different size. We show him two sticks and two kinds of curtain-rod rings. The child is to stack one type of ring on one stick and the other type of ring on the other stick. If he can do that, we can move on and set up three or four sticks, with curtain-rod rings in as many colors; later we can introduce different ring sizes. One time, we might have the child arrange the rings by color and the next time by size.

We also let him sort other things (pulling several smaller boxes out of a larger one, for example), so that the child will learn to distinguish between things that are identical and things that are different. We line up large and small spoons, chestnuts, walnuts, or peach pits, and later on peas, beans and cherry pits. We set up an assortment of buttons, colored strings, colored bands (cut into about 3-inch-long strips), or colored glass beads.

We cut the following shapes out of cardboard (two each): circles, ovals, crosses, stars, squares, rectangles, hexagons, and crescents. We glue one of each of these onto a strong piece of cardboard. Then we have the child match up the various shapes. Then the time has come to buy different, simple "inlay" toys. Toy stores carry a variety of coordination sets consisting of removable shapes of circles, triangles, diamonds, squares, ovals, hearts, etc.

Once the child can match forms, he is far enough advanced to handle pictures. Now we can buy all kinds of games for him, such as lotto games with simple, clear pictures, "snip 'n snap," picture dominoes and color dominoes, playing cards and play money. In all these games, we practice matching identical pictures or objects.

The stacking of rings on a stick is also the starting point for another sequence that we can employ along with those described above. In the case of the stationary stick, the child need only use one hand. Once he has mastered this operation, we can make the task a little more difficult so that he will have to use both hands. We give him a little stick and get the child to put the rings on the stick. If the stick is thin enough (such as the tiny rods from tinker-toy or erector sets), the child will also be able to spear spools of thread.

When he has learned to do that, we teach him to string large wooden beads. The larger the beads, the easier the task. Most toy stores have beads up to two inches in diameter; these are very good to start with. As string, we use a plastic laundry line or dental floss, because it is pliable. As the child's skill improves, we use smaller and smaller beads until we finally string up glass beads on thread with the help of a dull needle. Along the way, we call the child's attention to the various colors; we ask the child to use a certain color, or two alternate colors, etc.

The stringing of beads is the point of departure for sewing. We can give a normal child perforated cardboard pictures (the kind available in any toy store), and up to a certain point, the child will be able to do the required sewing by himself. Not so the retarded child. If you give him the same materials as the normal child, the retarded child will require far too much help to get anything done. This would tend to spoil the child and develop a habit of dependence in him; exactly the opposite of what we want. After all, we want the child to become self-reliant. Consequently we must give him the kinds of things to do that we can expect him to accomplish by himself after a suitable period of practice.

Once the child can string beads, we take a piece of cardboard and perforate it along the edges, using a plain office punch. The child can then string shoelaces through these big holes; later he can string yarn through them by means of a blunt needle.

Now we can buy a game called "The Old Woman Laced in a Shoe." This teaches children to lace their own shoes. It is generally sold with inserts to be put through the differently shaped windows.

If the child has mastered this operation, we can make the task of sewing a little more difficult by punching holes with a shoemaker's leather punch. This time we make the holes not only along the edges but also in the middle. We punch out two or three concentric circles or squares or a Swiss cross or some similar shape. If the child has learned this phase, we draw very simple pictures on the cardboard (a house, tree, cherries, bananas, spoons, birds, flowers, etc.). We punch holes along the outlines of these pictures and guide the child in stringing yarn through them. Only then are we far enough advanced to use sewing pictures from the toy store. In the meantime, years—not just months —have passed.

When the child can string large beads, he can also put forms and shapes into depressions. Stores sell various kinds of toys—both wooden and plastic—that are designed for this sole purpose. In the beginning, choose the very simple toys intended for smaller children; later, select increasingly complicated ones. After the child has acquired some skill in inserting, give him a pegboard with holes and wooden pegs of different colors. At first, we get the child to insert pegs of the same color in a row. Then we teach him to insert a simple pattern.

Very useful here are wooden instruction sets that feature perforated plates that can be connected with each other by means of small sticks. These are available in various sizes in most toy stores. We will not be needing any complicated parts for quite some time, so we can take the smallest set available. But we should pick the one that has the largest individual parts; our child will not be able to do anything with tiny parts until much later on. After all, in the beginning we are not interested in making toys with these sets. We merely want to teach the child to insert a small stick in each hole.

As soon as he can do that, we have him insert a little stick in a base plate, followed by a wheel, and on the latter's edge, another little stick. With this "handle" he can now turn the wheel; this is our first self-made toy. The child can use it to practice rotating movements. Now we teach the child how to make very simple objects. We concentrate only on those which we think he might be able to make by himself. Let's not allow our imagination to run away with us! Let's not be spurred too far by our own desire to play again. If we make wonderful little toy cars or cranes for the child, he will not be happy with simple objects which he could learn to make by himself.

We should therefore show the child how to make a ladder, for instance. He can climb up and down the ladder with his two fingers; this is good exercise for awkward little fingers, especially when combined with a simple rhyme. Or we might teach the child to make a tiny chair out of a plate into which he can insert four short sticks to constitute the four legs of the chair. Using longer sticks, he can make a table.

We put a doll of suitable size on the little chair, let it walk around the table, slip through under the chair, climb over the table and chair, and so on. Sometimes the child can be leading the doll around according to our instructions; at other times, we lead the doll around, allowing the child to observe us and then imitate us. There are vast possibilities for us here.

Hollow cubes were our first building material. If the

child has had a chance to learn how to connect objects by assembling these cubes, he can practice connecting objects with the help of building blocks. We need not specially recommend the use of building blocks; they are, after all, the one toy every child gets in the most varied designs; they are also put before the retarded child each day, mostly at the time when he is still in the playpen. This is quite correct. These blocks offer unlimited possibilities.

However, in respect to the free, unguided use of building blocks, we can make the same observation as on most other toys: creative imagination and hence creative play are rather feeble or entirely absent in mentally retarded children. We must also teach these children how to build, if they are to advance beyond the stage of simple, aimless handling of things in a reasonable period of time. Again we start with very simple structures. We teach the child to build a little shed around a toy animal, or a tunnel through which we roll a toy car, or roads for toy cars, or a tower, etc.

Children love to play with small colored plates and sticks that can be laid out in various patterns and designs. In the beginning, the retarded child does not know what to do with these plates and sticks. He takes a handful out of the box, lets them glide through his fingers, piles them up in a heap, puts them in his mouth, etc. We must teach the child how to use them correctly. In the beginning, we use this type of object to teach the child how to sort things by shape and color. Later we have the child line up a row made up of two different shapes, and we are happy to see how long he can make the row. Once he has mastered this, we come to a step for which our child will need certain training aids.

We now want to teach the child how to lay out various designs, the way children do in kindergarten. For the retarded child, however, we must break this task down into certain component parts, just as any other task. The mother should lay out simple designs on a sheet of paper, using various materials: on one sheet of paper, a table; on another sheet, a house; on additional sheets, a ladder, a tree, a cactus plant in a flowerpot, a Christmas tree, a toy wagon, and so on. The mother then outlines these shapes with a pencil and fills in the contours with colored pencil or crayon. Now we teach the child to lay his sticks and plates on the lines we have traced in advance. Later we use these lines as a kind of blueprint, and the child places his small pictures next to the picture on the paper. Finally we are far enough advanced so that our child can lay out his sticks and plates by himself, that is, without a sample pattern. Of course we will find that retarded children keep repeating the designs they have learned; they add little of their own, but we are happy with what little they can do.

Another variation of this toy is the hammer-and-nail set. Here the plates have holes and can easily be nailed to a special board with a light wooden hammer. This is a very good toy, because it furthers manual dexterity and because children like to hammer. Here, too, we advance step by step, as in the case of the layout toy. First we decorate the edge of the board with a design consisting of two alternating plate types. Then we hammer on the basis of the predrawn outline. After that we hammer next to the traced pattern, and finally we hammer without guide. If the child should give his creation a name—calling it, for instance, a "train," we name the characteristic features of the "train," such as the wheels, and so on.

Of course we also give the retarded child plenty of opportunity for free drawing; we hand him colored crayons and paper. The crayons should be of good quality, so that the points will not keep breaking. As for paper, we can just as well use the reverse side of folders, pads, or wrapping paper, rather than expensive drawing pads. There is no disputing the educational value of free drawing. But this is hard to handle in the case of the retarded child, because he scrawls on walls and furniture. Until he has learned to draw *only* on paper, the mother must keep an eye on the child playing with colored crayons.

The retarded child remains in the scrawling stage for years. He keeps scrawling back and forth on the paper, without any purpose and without being able or willing to name the object he has scrawled. Or he may draw one line and call it a dog. One minute later he may call the same line a railroad train. The child is totally satisfied with his work. There is no use trying to stimulate the child through criticism and comment. Nor does it help any if we allow the child enough time and hand him enough equipment to draw with and then leave him to his own devices. The retarded child cannot spontaneously move from one stage of development to the next within a reasonable period of time. This is why we must also teach him how to draw.

From aimless scrawling, we gradually try to get the child to the conscious fashioning of shapes. This is easier if we use crayons instead of ordinary colored pencils, because crayons make stronger and more brilliant traces. We have the child cover an entire sheet with crayon. If possible, this should be done with very wide, free, loose sweeps; the direction of the strokes should, if possible, be the same throughout. In this manner we are guiding the child in making harmonious motions whose colored, visible trace will make him happy. As soon as he can maintain a certain uniform stroke direction, we can put wide colored stripes on the paper, using straight, slanting, wavy, and other lines, as well as rays issuing from a central point or from several centers. The child can make circles around a center or he can draw them freely, one running into the other. The possibilities here are tremendous.

We also try to get the child to draw "patterns." That is to say, we want the child to repeat regularly recurring decorative designs: two lines and a circle in between, for a starter. We also teach him how to trace the outlines of simple shapes with a colored crayon: here we can use a building block or one of the layout plates or the molds used for cooky baking. Then we ask the child to fill in the contours with crayon. Children like to do this because it is easy and produces a pretty picture that they can give away or hang up in their rooms. Only after the child has mastered all this will it make any sense to buy picture fill-in books, because these contain much more complicated forms.

We also teach the child the "language of shapes," that is, the manner in which things in the environment are usually drawn on paper—a house, a tree, a man, etc. After awhile, the child will love to draw the shapes and forms he has been taught. He will also add some of his own. Each child's drawings differ from those of the next child. We will be happy to note that drawing offers our retarded children a chance to express what is inside them. This is to be welcomed, especially in those children who find it difficult to express themselves in words because they are far behind in their speech development.

Painting with water colors is another activity that is good for the retarded child and gives him pleasure. Naturally this is not easy to do at home. The retarded child cannot use commercially available paintboxes, because the process of color transfer onto paper is too complicated for the child.

It is best to buy paints in tubes and dissolve the paint in small cups containing water. Each little cup or bowl should have its own thick, soft brush; in other words, one brush for each color. This eliminates the need for rinsing the brush (too difficult for the child), and the colors remain pure.

The retarded child, too, loves to dip the thick, soft brush into the colored liquid and is happy when he can see the visible trace he has made on the paper. As in the case of drawing with crayon, the important thing in painting, initially, is not so much *what* the child paints, as *how* he paints. He should be pleased by the large colored surfaces covering his sheet of paper, by the various multicolored shapes and stripes and other designs he can create. Retarded children tend to prefer to keep scratching and scrawling with the pencil. Painting on large sheets of paper can be a good remedy here.

It is understandable why very few parents let their children do this; after all, "accidents" are frequent, and many things are splashed with paint.

Clay modeling is easier than painting in the home. The retarded child loves to model and knead at a rather early age, fashioning the clay into all kinds of odd shapes.

Sometimes we get the child to roll the clay or plasticine into a sausage shape. Many a retarded child is tireless in his output of long, very long, sausages. Then we teach him to make pretzels, cigars, bottles, and the like, from these sausage shapes. We also practice rotating movements with the hands, making a ball between the two palms; this leads to further shapes and combinations.

A child experiences the same kind of pleasure when playing with sand. This material also evokes activity in mentally retarded children. Even the restless child is fascinated by sand, and occupies himself with the sandbox longer than with any other activity. The manifold possibilities offered by wet sand cause the all-too-passive child, as well as the nonconcentrating child, to try new things. Of course, this kind of play is proper only after the child realizes that sand is not to be put in the mouth.

It is good for the retarded child's dexterity to help the mother with household chores. Dusting and wiping, carrying things, watering the flowers in the garden with a little watering can, replacing the water in a vase, washing potatoes or beets—all these activities develop his skills as well as his character. This gives the child's personality a lift.

In time you can make the child responsible for certain minor tasks; he will thus have his own chores, like other members of the family. If you think hard enough, you will find many things—many everyday household functions—which even a severely retarded child can perform. Of course you could do it all much faster yourself, especially in the beginning. But do not be reluctant to spend the time teaching the child such chores; fifteen or so years from now you will be glad that you trained your retarded child to make himself useful around the house from the very beginning.

You cannot teach your child all this at one time. It will probably take several years before he has learned the things discussed in this chapter. A child's reduced capabilities result in a considerable delay in the rate of development. A retarded child does not acquire new knowledge and new skills in one fast sweep: he advances with the tiniest of steps.

Almost every sentence in this chapter describes such a little step, the mastery of which may take weeks, months, and even years. Be sure the child really knows a certain step before moving on to the next step. The child must have a chance to remain on a certain level until he has outgrown it. On the other hand, do not hold him back on a certain level simply because this is easier—because it is more convenient to have the child play with the same things all the time. This means that you must at all times guide your child toward the kind of activity he needs to engage in at a particular moment—the kind of activity that will enable him to advance. Thus the child will always be happy when you give him your time, and you will be grateful to find out how much even a retarded child can do.

17

Walking

ALL OF THE EXERCISES mentioned so far help us stimulate the child's attention, his ability to concentrate, his capacity for observation, his ambition, his creativity, and his manual dexterity. But this is not enough. We must also try to make the child more mobile, to get him to acquire mobility with his entire body.

If the child does not move his limbs at all, there is reason to suspect that he is paralyzed. Take him to a pediatrician. If the child holds an arm or a leg or the head in the same peculiar position all the time, go to a doctor or to the clinic of a children's hospital. The doctor will show you simple exercises that you can do with the child daily at home; such exercises can help correct these and other defects in posture. Perhaps the doctor will advise you to go to a physiotherapist who will then regularly exercise your child. This specialist will best know how to get the child to make the kinds of movements he cannot perform by himself.

Many retarded children do not have trouble learning to

walk because they are paralyzed, but because movement is
also controlled by the brain and the latter is not properly
developed.

Don't let your child lie in his crib or bed for years; you
will wait in vain for him to learn how to walk. Even if the
child should be happy in his bed, it is better for you to
put him in the playpen for the whole day from a certain
age onward. Then you can hope that the child will learn
to prop himself up, especially when you help. Maybe his
natural walking instinct will develop, after all, causing him
to pull himself along.

Retarded children with very large heads always learn to
walk much later. They have trouble keeping their balance
and for this reason, do not stand up to begin with. These
children have to be stood on their legs time and again, so
that they can gradually find a way of keeping their relatively large heads balanced. It is a laborious process to
teach them how to walk, because they keep losing their
balance and toppling over unexpectedly. Like all other
retarded children, they react slowly; this means that they
cannot break the fall with their hands. They fall over like
a sack. This is a frightening sight for any mother. In teaching the child how to walk, we must move out of the way
any furniture against which the child might fall and injure
himself. But it would be a mistake to give up all attempts
at walking out of fear that the child might fall, or perhaps
to prevent him from walking by himself if he should so
desire. Children must also learn how to fall. It is better for
them to learn this while they are still small; they are
closer to the floor.

We need not have these and other worries in the case of

Mongoloids. They fall as softly as kittens and rarely hurt themselves. Later on, when they get older, they do not get scraped knees or palms as often as their normal contemporaries.

Various aids have been designed for children who learn to walk later in life. These aids are useless and sometimes even harmful for normal children, but are often helpful for retarded children.

If the child can sit by himself but cannot walk as yet, we can use a hassock with wheels. The child straddles this four-wheeled hassock or footstool, and, so to speak, paddles his way forward with both legs by pushing with his legs against the floor. In front, the hassock or footstool has two handles that the child can grip with his hands. The handles are made in the shape of a horse's head, a snail, or a doe's head. In most cases, the children love their little horse head or snail and like to practice with it.

As soon as the child can stand by himself with some assistance, we can put him in a walker. The latter consists of four rods terminating in a top and a bottom ring. The top ring is just wide enough for us to slip the child through; the bottom ring is considerably wider and has four little wheels. The child leans against the top ring with his arms, thus moving the entire device; he must therefore run along with it. Since the child cannot sit down in this device, the mother must be sure to take the child out before he gets tired.

We might also use a small chair on wheels; the child can hold on to the chair and push it ahead of himself. The chair should have rather widely spaced legs and it should not be so light that it will fall over as a result of the child's awkward movements.

Of course, the mother should keep trying to lead the child around the floor herself until he has learned to walk, but the child learns better when he is supported by a walker or a chair. When the child supports himself on a chair, for instance, he is entirely on his own; he learns to correct his movements to prevent losing his balance. But when he is led by the mother, he tends to rely too much on being supported and held, regardless of how he walks and moves.

Some children can walk but they still sit around too much. Don't let your child sit all day. Keep calling him to come to you; try to get him to walk, at least across the room in order to reach a toy or a piece of candy. Don't carry him, once he can walk. Take him for a walk as soon as possible; this will not only strengthen his legs but will also expand his field of vision and investigation.

If the child can walk, play little games of skill with him. Teach him to climb stairs and to walk backwards. Draw a chalk line on the floor and let the child walk on that line. Set up some building blocks and have the child walk between them without knocking them over. Put a broomstick across two building blocks and have the child step over it; you can also use a taut skipping rope. But don't forget that jumping is more difficult; your child will not learn that until much later. Let him climb a small stepladder. Teach him to climb on the chair, under the chair, under the table, etc.

The child will have to concentrate even more if he has to carry something while walking. Have him carry a tray on which you have placed a box; the child can then try to walk around without having the box fall off the tray. Later we can put two building blocks on the tray, which the child must not let fall over. Teach him to carry a glass of water to the table without spilling any. Have him carry a small potato or a little ball in a soup spoon. This is even more difficult when the child has a spoon in each hand. Then let him carry a little bell without making it tinkle, etc.

Many mentally retarded children like rhythm. Let your child "march" to the rhythm of a children's song; let him clap his hands, walk, jump, hop—slowly or rapidly—in rhythm; let him clap softly or loudly, following the way you clap your hands. In place of hand-clapping, you can also use a small drum, a tambourine or similar instrument. There are many rhythmic games that will be good for the child and make him happy. Singing and music are important in the education of retarded children. We will come back to this topic later.

18

Speech

MOST MENTALLY retarded children are also more or less far behind in their speech development. Many parents realize that their child is different only when they notice he cannot manage to speak at an age when other children chatter happily.

If your child does not start talking at the proper time, take him to an ear, nose, and throat specialist. The latter is best equipped to determine whether your child is hard of hearing. If a child cannot hear human speech properly, he will naturally have difficulty learning it.

Perhaps the doctor will discover other organic defects such as malformation or impairments in the oral cavity or in the pharyngeal space, abnormal position of teeth, etc. These and other defects are often found in mentally retarded children. But generally it is not these minor or major organic defects which are responsible for slow speech development. Normal children can also have such deformations which hinder them in speaking as clearly as might be expected at their age. Speech therapy can help to eliminate minor organic defects completely.

In retarded children, however, speech retardation is a consequence of general mental debility. These children lack the preconditions and prerequisites for the acquisition of speech—that is, spontaneous drive, interest, the desire for productive imitation, and attention. We must place special emphasis on the development of speech in these children. In the beginning, we are not so concerned with correcting isolated, particularly irritating, errors of pronunciation: what we usually have to do is to help the child build up his speech from scratch.

As soon as the child can understand, or begins to understand, what we are saying, we try to get him to speak; at first we merely have the child imitate sounds made by us. On suitable occasions we have him imitate animal sounds that we have produced, such as *"moo-moo," "bow-wow," "baa-baa,"* etc. Then we have the child imitate, along with us, the sounds of a railroad train or a car or the sound of a pair of scissors being snapped shut, etc.

In this connection, we might make the observation that the child is as awkward in moving his mouth as he is in moving his hands. Many mentally retarded children have difficulty in moving their tongues and cannot properly control the movement of their lips. We must practice these skills with them, as with any other skill. It is good exercise for the tongue if we spread a little honey on the upper lip and the child can lick with his tongue. We do the same thing with the lower lip, first in one corner, then in the other.

We can further the control of mouth movements by

means of blowing. We have the child blow out candles or we get him to blow a cotton ball across the table or we have him blow soap bubbles with a straw. Children generally love these and other games and like to practice with them.

As soon as he can, we try to get the child to repeat individual words after us. Again and again, we try to get the child to say "Mama" to us and "Daddy" to his father, to give the names of his siblings, and to name the objects with which he comes in contact. Words which we want the child to learn must be repeated day after day. Here we must make sure that we always use the same words for the same things. When we dress or undress the child, we always say "Shoe"; we do not alternatingly use "Shoesey-Wooseys," "Sandals," "Booties," and so on—otherwise the child will learn none of these expressions. When we feed the child, we always use the word "Meal"; we do not alternatingly say "Lunch" or "Supper." We try to teach the child to say "Come" when he wants us to come over, and "Goodbye" when he or others leave.

As in all other aspects, your child follows you in speech —to the extent permitted by his capacities. You must speak to the child clearly and distinctly. Your speech is the model here; be sure it is a good model.

As soon as the child begins to repeat individual words after you, he will also pick up expressions which you did not teach him intentionally. This is good, for the child is showing that he can, on his own, remember and use individual details. Be sure that he learns only good expressions. Don't use ugly words, insulting words, or curses. Don't think the child is not listening or paying attention. In the case of the retarded child—as in that of the normal one—we can never exactly be sure of what he happens to be paying attention to at any particular moment. Remember that it is much more difficult to break a retarded child of a bad habit than to teach him a good habit. If, in anger, you call your child names that should not be repeated, do not be surprised if he uses similar expressions toward you or other persons. The difference between a child who speaks politely and in a friendly fashion and the child who speaks a rough language often does not lie in his character but in the example set for him by his environment.

Teach your child the standard expressions that he will need every day, such as "How do you do?" "Good-bye," "Please," "Thank you," etc. Train him to answer recurring questions in the same way at all times, such as giving his name when asked, or replying to the question "How are you?" with a "Fine, thank you."

It would be wrong to teach the child baby talk which would be difficult to discontinue later on. It sounds strange when the mother of a boy who looks ten years old says that he has to go "make pee-pee," or wash his little "hand-sey-wandseys" and put on his "shoesey-wooseys." It is better to teach the child the correct expression from the very beginning.

The retarded child must not only be taught how to speak; he must also be taught how to keep silent. Some children must be taught how to be silent even before they can speak. These are the children who have a tendency to keep babbling. Babbling is in itself a useful activity: it is good speech practice that every healthy baby engages in eagerly. The healthy child loses his desire for babbling as he learns to talk. In the retarded child, whose speech does not develop as rapidly, babbling can become a habit which he will keep for years. The more monotonous this becomes, the more it loses the very meaning and significance assigned to it by nature: if the child keeps saying the same sounds and sound combinations over and over again, he will not be practicing anything new.

Regardless of whether the child is still babbling or already talking, he must learn that there are times when he must be silent: when grownups are conversing, when brothers or sisters are doing their homework, or when Father is taking his afternoon nap. This kind of consideration is good not only for the person receiving it but also for the person giving it—the retarded child. The ability to keep quiet is a part of good manners.

The retarded child, too, likes our familiar old children's verses. You should recite such rhymes for him often. In time, the child will try to say the words after you, even though he does not understand their meaning; in the end, he will even be able to recite one or the other of these rhymes from memory. There are mentally retarded children whose memory is good and who memorize verses with the greatest of ease.

These children are particularly happy when they can accompany rhythmic talking with suitable movements. This is why we play with them the so-called finger games which mothers play with normal babies. This is not only good talking practice, but also promotes mobility. If you do not remember enough rhymes and games from your own childhood, you can buy one of the many books available that contain well-known childhood rhymes or finger games.

The same is true of songs. Sing for your child as often

as you feel like it; this will be good for both of you. Every mentally retarded child likes to listen to singing or other kinds of music; all listen joyfully, many of them with great perseverance. There are also retarded children who have a good ear for music; some may be on a very low mental level and still have a remarkably good ear.

They sing with voices as clear as bells, and they remember every tune, even before they can utter a comprehensible word. Others cannot sing at all. Between these two extremes, we have all those gradations of musical capability which we also find among normal people. However, even those children who cannot sing are favorably affected by music; they grasp the mood of the music and can thus be influenced constructively. When the child is excited, he can often be soothed by a song or soft music.

Music that is made in the mentally retarded child's presence is more significant to him than music transmitted via some piece of technical equipment. Use radio and television carefully. Even the best female voice, transmitted, can never replace the song sung by the mother herself. Her singing—no matter how imperfect—projects feelings and moods that shape the child's emotions and have a good effect on the relationship between mother and child. If you constantly turn on radio and television, your child will tend to become inattentive, listen with only half an ear, and fail to concentrate. In the case of the retarded child, this is particularly serious, since he inclines toward these faults from the very outset.

Even mentally retarded children can sing delightfully and heart-warmingly. Though we may be very happy to listen to their singing, we must let them know that there are times and places when they must not sing—on the streetcar, at mealtime, or when visiting. We must also see to it that the child does not develop the habit of coming out with a monotonous singsong that has nothing to do with music.

If your child is musically gifted, it is best for you to refrain from giving him any of the cheap instruments you can get in the toy store and with which the child cannot possibly make a clear sound—such as blaring children's trumpets or toy pianos which are out of tune to begin with. Such instruments can ruin the child's ear and do not develop his sense of the beautiful. Every instrument you give your child should have a clear sound; this is why it is best to buy these instruments in a music store. Besides, the mentally retarded child can get along quite well without musical instruments for many years.

19

Eating

EATING AND DRINKING are complicated operations. We must
realize from the very beginning that we are going to have
a lot of trouble and hard work until the child has mastered
these skills to the extent desired by us and demanded by
the civilized world. The first instructions should be given
in strict privacy—not at the table with the rest of the
family. It is best for the retarded child and for the other
family members to feed the child before the family gathers
around the table. This will give you a chance to concentrate on the child and afterward devote yourself more fully
and calmly to your other loved ones. It is not good for the
family when the retarded child's behavior causes excitement at every meal. While you are paying attention to
your husband and your other children, the best you can
do is "shovel" the food down the retarded child's throat,
but you cannot teach him how he should be eating.

In teaching the retarded child how to feed himself, we
must expect many a mishap. Child, mother, table, chair,
and floor should be properly protected. Plastic table-

cloths, doilies, and aprons are better than the kind that only adds to your laundry. In the beginning—and possibly for a long time—the child will keep smearing his face and hands as he tries to feed himself. Keep a wet washcloth and a towel within reach, so that you will not have to jump up every time there is a mishap. This only creates an atmosphere of restlessness.

It is important to have peace, quiet, and good cheer at every meal. This is doubly important in the case of the retarded child, because every meal has a double objective for him: he must be well nourished and he must learn how to eat and drink.

20

Drinking

THERE IS a vast difference between sucking from a bottle and drinking from a cup. Sucking is an instinctive act that the child takes up shortly after birth because it feels the urge to do so; drinking, on the other hand, is a skill that must be learned.

This task, too, must be broken down into its component parts for the retarded child. Our first goal here is to teach the child to swallow a liquid without prior sucking.

If we take a child, sitting upright, and put small quantities of liquid into his mouth with a teaspoon, most of the liquid will run out again. But if the mother holds the child in her arms in a slightly reclined position, the child will instinctively swallow the content of the teaspoon. Through practice, we can get the child to the point where he can swallow the liquid from the teaspoon while sitting upright.

Once the child can do this without major difficulty, we can begin to teach him how to drink. Instead of the spoon, we now put a cup to his mouth. The cup should be only one quarter full. It should be inclined only far enough so that the child will get one small swallow at a time. Do not flood the child with liquid so that he will swallow the wrong way and become scared. Don't forget that the child is not yet accustomed to swallowing rapidly in succession. We must give him time, and we can increase the speed only gradually.

Once the child has learned this operation, we can try to get him to help hold the cup. After awhile he will probably want to hold the cup himself. We welcome this desire enthusiastically. We do not spare praise here, though for a long time it may be necessary for us to help as tactfully and unobtrusively as we can. In this stage, also, the cup should never be quite full, because it is much harder to get a small quantity of liquid from a full cup than from one that is only half full.

Cups with one handle are not suitable for retarded children. Their little fingers cannot grasp the handle; neither strength nor skill enable the retarded child to control a cup with one hand. It is better to give the child a cup without handles and to train him to grasp the cup with both hands.

Later on it would be a good idea to get the child accustomed to drinking with a straw. This comes in handy when you are away from home; most drinks for children are served with a straw. Once the child has mastered the use of the straw, he can drink much more tidily. But we must watch out that he does not blow into the drink. "Blowing bubbles" with a straw in the drink is a favorite occupation, even for normal children. But the retarded child cannot understand why we should laugh when he does this at home and scold when he does the same thing outside.

21

Meals

SOME RETARDED CHILDREN refuse to take solid food at an age when other children eat the same food as their parents. They do not want to chew, though they have enough healthy teeth; the mother must prepare all dishes in the form of mush, or the child will not touch them. This gets very complicated and is not good for the child in the long run, because chewing is a necessary activity. Reluctance to chew is a widespread evil of our day and age. Today's normal children and even adults are often too lazy to chew. Doctors and dentists have much to say on this subject. Many of our retarded children, however, find chewing exceedingly troublesome. We must try hard from the very beginning to teach them the habit of chewing. But how?

Some mothers give their children dry bread crusts to chew during teething, to facilitate the process. Whether this really makes teething any easier or not, it cannot be denied that these children do not develop as negative an attitude toward chewing as those who are never given anything to chew. Aimless chewing seems to be the first step here. Keep putting small pieces of zwieback or cookies in the baby's hands. Most of them will chew on these, not only because they like the sweet taste, but because they also like the sound of the crunching.

To get the child used to solid food, we start off with dishes that are not mushy but that require only very little in the way of chewing—a sort of mashing inside the mouth. A good example here is milk toast. Of course we select only those foods whose taste the little one will like, such as a small piece of light biscuit that more or less melts on the tongue. Let us remember that not all children like the taste of sweet things; some prefer spicy flavors. There are children who would rather chew on a slice of salami than on a piece of zwieback. We can make solid food more attractive for these children if we first give them a small piece of hamburger meat or perhaps tiny meatballs.

In the beginning, we give the child only small quantities of solid foods, at best perhaps only a mouthful. We do this at the start of the meal when the child is still hungry. After he has nicely swallowed the solid food, he may eat his favorite mush to his heart's content. We gradually increase the quantity of solid food; little by little, the child will get used to it, especially when the mother is calm about the whole thing.

In general, a retarded child should get the same food as a normal child. If you are in doubt as to whether you are feeding your child properly, see a pediatrician. Change the customary type of diet only on doctor's orders. A one-sided diet may harm the child.

Like anyone else, the retarded child will have his food preferences and dislikes. This is no cause for alarm. As in any other case, we must try to see to it that our child does not become too choosy. This goes without saying. Still, we do not want to insist on having the child eat something he definitely does not like—something to which he has a definite aversion. Let us not overemphasize the point; let us not make an issue of it; let us tactfully pass over it. We know that there are well-educated and well-adjusted adults who cannot overcome their aversion to certain foods.

In training, it is not only the *what* that counts, but also the *how;* it is not only important to consider what your child eats but also how he eats. In this respect, too, we must constantly and gradually increase our requirements. In the beginning, we will be glad if the child lets himself be fed like a good little boy or girl, opens the mouth nicely as the spoon approaches, and closes it again.

During feeding, let us try to keep the small face from becoming smeared as best we can. Some mothers feed their children in a manner reminiscent of a mason slapping mortar against a wall. Later on, it is hard to teach these children to eat neatly. It is better to feed the child carefully and to let him know from the beginning that food belongs *in* the mouth, not some place near it. Later, the child will be more likely to try to achieve the same goal.

From the very outset we must get the child accustomed to remaining seated until the meal is over. It is not good to allow the child to walk around and play between courses. Nor should you let him put his hands into the plate. But if he does do this in an attempt to move some of the food to his mouth, welcome this sign of purposeful and directed thinking. We should be pleased by this drive for

independence, but we should make it clear to the child
that he can do a better job with a spoon.

Before we can expect a retarded child to handle a spoon
by himself, we must give him plenty of time for preliminary exercises. We let him play in the sand and have
him fill his little pail with a small shovel, or we have him
shovel the sand from one pail to another. We let him
spoon peas or beans or rice from one container into another. For practice, we use various types of saucers and
plates, because each kind requires a different movement.

A spoon handle is a very small object. Perhaps your child
is not yet able to handle such a delicate item the way you
would want him to. Things might go easier if you fastened
the spoon handle to the handle of a wooden ladle, using
Scotch tape or some such means. This will give the child
a better and surer grip.

Eating, however, requires not only the handling of the
spoon; it also means hitting the mouth on target. We practice these two operations separately, because we can teach
the retarded child only one function at a time. To hit the
mouth correctly, we use a spoon dipped into a little honey
or moistened granulated sugar. In this manner, every
successful attempt at the same time leads to a reward. Of
course, his face and perhaps even hair may become a bit
sticky in the process, but this should not dismay us or
cause us to drop our practice sessions. In the case of many
a retarded child whose perfect table manners we admire,
the mother can still remember the honey-smeared little
face that she washed several times a day for a long time.

In time, we encourage the child to hold the spoon during
meals, and we guide his hand so that he will be moving

the food from the plate to his mouth. If we repeat this often enough, we will note that we no longer need guide the little hand all the way; gradually we can leave the spoon entirely in the child's hand. Of course, the movements will not yet be perfect; they will be clumsy, unsure, and jerky. In this phase we must expect that the child will smear himself, the table, and perhaps also the surrounding area. But we must not give up. If the child has learned to feed himself with a spoon, he has learned something important.

Of course, we ought to take some precautionary measures. We use a plate with a high rim such as we get for babies, because it is easier to get food on the spoon from such a plate and because there is less danger of spilling. We also want to see to it that the child does not play around or dawdle during the meal. If he is through eating, we remove the plate before the child has a chance to play with it. Thus the child finds out that certain things are done at certain times and not to be done at others.

Remember that it is easier to spoon mushy dishes than entirely liquid ones and that pudding and jello have a tendency to slip off the spoon. Don't get angry if your child manages to eat mashed potatoes quite well but still keeps spilling soup. Don't scold; don't say, "You could, if you'd only try." Have patience. Your child will learn to master this difficult task, too, if you will give him enough chance for calm practice.

Whether or not we teach the child to use an implement with which he can shove food onto the spoon depends on the child's condition. If he generally has a good appetite and looks forward to his meals, he will want to use such a device. Such children like to handle an additional implement that enables them to eat their favorite dish faster. But we must be aware that the use of a second utensil is a big undertaking. Now the child must perform two different operations at the same time: he must scoop up the food with one hand and at the same time push with the other. If we think that this would help our child, we can teach him to use this shoving utensil in a manner similar to the way we taught him the use of the spoon.

If the child can drink from a glass quite well and eat with the spoon so that he no longer needs constant assistance but only supervision, the time has come to let him join the rest of the family at the table. Make it clear to the child that this is a step forward, a reward for his hard work, and that he must now really do his best. If he does not behave properly, he will lose this privilege.

Now the family can be of great help. Every member should be aware of this—not only the father and the mother; brothers and sisters should be prepared for this moment. Everyone should be happy that the family is now far enough advanced to gather as a whole. Let everyone be ready to do his or her part toward the success of this undertaking. Help from the other siblings will come in the form of occasional small services, but mainly by way of the good example they set. The retarded child will behave the way you behave at the table. If you are excited and unfriendly, he will become fidgety and "pesty." Make sure that you help your child along through your example.

There are retarded children—even severely retarded

ones—whose table manners are so good that they blend in anywhere, even in a restaurant. In trying to achieve all this, we are not seeking to conceal the child's condition from ourselves and from others; we are trying to equip the child to move among people without being offensive.

22

Undressing and Dressing

IT MAY SEEM STRANGE that we mention undressing first and dressing afterward. There is a reason for this: it is much easier to undress than to dress. This is readily understandable if we realize how much easier it is, for instance, to slip off a shoe or pull off a pair of stockings than to put them on. The retarded child must first be taught the easier operation.

Most children practice undressing without Mother's prompting, often even against her wishes. You put a child in the garden or start taking him for a walk on a cold day, and he promptly takes his cap off and strips off his mittens —while Mother comes to a slow boil. There are children— including retarded ones—who keep doing this over and over again and make a game out of it: they take the cap off and Mother puts it back on again. Annoying as this may be, it does have the advantage of getting the child to learn how to take off some pieces of clothing.

But from here it is a long and hard road to the skill of undressing and dressing completely or even only partially. It takes normal children several years to learn this. The retarded child needs much more time, both because of his mental retardation and because of the clumsiness of his movements. Moreover, some of these children have a tendency to take off various pieces of clothing at the wrong time; here, again, they must learn that there is a time and a place for everything.

The child should also learn the sequence of the various individual operations, so that the entire process can be simplified. He must, for instance, be taught that shoes come off before pants and that buttons must be unbuttoned before a shirt or blouse can be taken off.

Undressing and dressing chiefly consist of the following operations: pulling down and pulling outward; tucking in and pulling out. While the child is still completely helpless, the mother does all this. She should keep saying the term for the operation she has just performed: "Pull off," "Pull up," "Tuck in," "Take off." In this manner, the child will gradually connect certain items of clothing with certain activities.

When you undress the child, always do it in the same sequence. Get your child to help you in the process. Guide his hand in taking off shoes and socks after you have pulled them over the heels. Let the child help you slide his pants over his hips, and after sitting down, pull them off altogether. It is much harder to take off clothing over the head; try this at first with loosely fitting clothes that are easier to remove. It is generally better to practice with clothing that is a little too large for the child—in the hope that later he will be able to handle tighter-fitting clothing.

We can familiarize the child with the functions of pull-

ing down and pulling up by sewing a wide strip of cloth
(or a handkerchief) together at the ends. The child should
then slide the cloth over his body in both directions (of
course over the clothing he happens to be wearing at the
time).

To teach a normal child how to undress and dress, it
suffices to have the child do this once in the course of the
day, but the retarded child needs intensive practice to
learn this. We must give him a chance to practice several
times a day. We also get special pieces of clothing for
practice. We need a bag (colored cotton would be best),
and we put a large hole for the neck in the closed end of
the bag and large armholes in the sides. This is our training
aid for the preliminary exercises of taking off and putting
on shirt, blouse, coat, or similar pieces of clothing. Then
we take another bag and put two large holes in the bottom
for the legs; now we practice taking off and putting on the
pants. Once the child can take off and put on these large,
simple, loose items, we start him practicing with his own
clothing.

Buttons, snap buttons, hooks, and zippers are difficult
for children to handle. The best preliminary practice for
buttoning is playing with various games that require the
insertion of a little stick or some such object, as described
in the chapter on general training.

When the child has learned to insert variously shaped
objects into depressions or small sticks into holes, we make
a button frame. We take an old picture frame and sew one
piece of cloth each on two opposite sides so that they will
overlap a little along the center line of the frame. Where
they overlap, we sew large buttons along the edge of one

of the cloth pieces: we make the corresponding button-holes in the edge of the other piece of cloth. Once the child has learned buttoning on the frame, we put his own sweater or coat on the table in front of him and let him practice buttoning that. Only after he has mastered this step do we guide him in buttoning the jacket he may have on.

Now we take another practice frame, and instead of but-tons, we sew on snap buttons, in order to practice this skill, too. Then we take a third frame on which we provide the piece of cloth with round eyelets, so that we can prac-tice lacing. Later we can use this third frame to practice the tying of string. But this is a complicated operation; the child must first reach a certain level of development before he can try this.

After the child has learned to put on his shoes, we face the problem of distinguishing between the right and left shoe. A colored marker attached to the inside of one shoe will indicate that this shoe belongs on a particular foot.

Of course, we teach the child to lay out his clothes in a certain sequence and to care for them properly.

Learning how to dress is a more painstaking and la-borious affair. Your child's achievement in this respect depends not only on your endeavors but also on the degree of your child's handicap. This, by the way, applies to all other skills. There are children who never learn how to dress; others can dress themselves part of the way; others cease to require any assistance whatever after some years.

The child may be able to dress and undress up to a point, though very, very slowly. We must take this slow-ness into consideration in our training. A child that is constantly hurried along will soon lose any desire for further efforts; scolding does more harm than good here. We should always make it a rule to allow much more time for dressing than is generally customary. As a matter of fact, this rule should apply in everything you do for your retarded child—that is, of course, in anything in which you expect him to participate or help you. At this point we might recall another rule: don't do anything for the child that he can do for himself.

Try to get the child interested in his outward appearance and to arouse his pride in something new or pretty. A little vanity can be a great help in our attempts to get the child to handle his clothes carefully. It may help to let the child look at himself in a mirror and see how nice he looks with his clean suit and friendly face; occasionally we might let him also see how ugly he looks, standing there with a soiled suit or a mean look.

Make sure the child is always properly dressed for the weather. Retarded children do not move around as much and always get cold faster than other children. Many retarded children are particularly prone to catching cold. Very often they cannot tell you that they are cold, even if they have learned to talk, because they are not aware of exactly what it is they are feeling. They feel uncomfortable and become "pesty" or they start crying and wet themselves. It is up to the mother to find out whether the child is cold.

Whether the child runs around with his legs bare or covered should not depend on fashion but on his comfort. On the other hand, don't bundle your child up too much if there is no reason to do so. A child inclined toward clumsiness to begin with will only become clumsier when he is too warm, and a fidgety child will become more restless when he perspires. Warm clothing should leave the child as much freedom of movement as light clothing. If your child is wearing almost as many shorts and T-shirts as an onion has skins, he will probably be highly restricted in his movements; this will keep him from making himself warmer in the natural way, by moving around more.

23

Cleanliness

ON THE SUBJECT of cleanliness, we can make the same observations for retarded children as for normal children: they like to take a bath but they do not like to wash themselves. Most children are happy in the tub and therefore quite receptive to guidance. For instance, at a very early stage in his development, we can encourage the child to hold the soap and to put it back in the dish, not into the water. We can also guide him in washing himself. This task is made easier when we give the child a terry-cloth mitten rather than a face flannel, because the mitten is not lost as easily. We teach the child how to rub the soap on the mitten, how to lather himself, and how to rinse himself off —and we teach him how to resist the temptation to play around instead of getting the job done.

Taking a bath is such a big chore for the child that he will probably need our help for many years to come— perhaps forever—if he is to achieve cleanliness.

On the other hand, we can and should teach most retarded children how to wash their hands and faces. Here, habituation must start early. In the course of the day, the child must be given the firm understanding that he is to wash at certain times; he will then accept this as something natural. It must be made absolutely clear to the child that he is not to come to breakfast unwashed, that he must wash his hands before every meal, and that he must at least wash face and hands before going to bed. We put a little footstool in front of the sink; the child can step on the stool and will then be at the right height to reach down into the bowl.

Brushing the teeth can be quite a chore for both mother and child. Many retarded children strongly resist having their teeth brushed. Because they do not open the mouth properly and do not hold still, some of the softer portions of the mouth inevitably come into rough contact with the bristles of the toothbrush, and this makes the whole operation even more unpopular. The task is particularly difficult with the child whose tongue is too large; he finds it hard to keep the tongue behind the teeth. This is the case with most Mongoloids.

It is a big help if we succeed in getting the child to perform this function by himself. Here it is best for the mother to stand behind the child, to look into the mirror with the child, and to guide his hand. This eliminates the unpleasant aspect of passive suffering, and in time this becomes another habit that the child acquires for himself. This should really be our goal here.

Dental care is particularly important in retarded children. Many have bad teeth to begin with. If we add the reluctance to chew, there is even more danger of dental disorders. We must try to forestall this as much as possible through proper care of teeth.

Up to a point, we can also teach the child to brush and comb his hair, but Mother will always have to add the finishing touches. Many retarded children could never be expected to part their hair or braid their hair into pigtails.

24

Toilet Training

THIS IS a very big job for the child, because it requires the control of bodily functions that actually occur subconsciously. There are ambitious mothers who hold their three- or four-month-old babies over the pot; we know from experience that these children "mind" no sooner than others whose training was started later. Even the normal child takes several years to learn how to control his bladder and intestinal functions. The retarded child, of course, will need much more time.

We need not overemphasize this problem vis-à-vis the child; we would not be helping the child if we did. Control of elimination is no more and no less important than, for instance, the acquisition of good table manners. Most mothers get far more excited when the child wets his pants than when he spills a glass of milk. This is not good.

We must teach our child the use of the toilet seat in as objective and calm a manner as we teach him the use of the spoon or the toothbrush. No mother will scold her retarded child for not being able to use a spoon as yet;

she must refrain from scolding her child if he cannot use the pot as yet. With calm, patience, and perseverance, our child will learn control of elimination much better than through scolding and punishment. Every retarded child capable of acquiring any knowledge or skill at all will in time also learn how to use the toilet seat; some take a long time, some take even longer.

Toilet training takes years. Progress is not constant. There may be times when you will get the impression that your child is making almost no progress. You must also expect setbacks. It may happen that a quite nicely "housebroken" child will again start to wet and perhaps even soil not only his bed but also his pants.

Such relapses may have psysiological causes such as intestinal disorders, a cold, or some minor irritation that makes the child uncomfortable and impairs his attentiveness.

Emotional discomfort can also lead to relapses. We can see this in the case of children of whom more is demanded than they can possibly accomplish, no matter how badly they may want to. We observe this in children who are afraid of something, or who adopt a negative attitude of spite, or feel that they are not sufficiently loved and accepted.

Scolding and punishment are practically useless here. In general, they only make the situation worse. Don't lose patience if your child behaves the way he used to when he was younger. Don't get angry with him. It may be that the child is begging for more love and attention by acting in this unpleasant manner. Start all over again—with undismayed calm, with unshakable patience, and with the proof of the love that you will in reality never lose toward your child, not even when he does things much worse than wetting his pants. Relapses in toilet training must be anticipated, even in normal children—how much more so, then, in retarded children!

We should change diapers frequently from the very beginning, so that the child will be dry as often and as long as possible and thus experience the pleasure of this condition. Children whose diapers are changed at long intervals become accustomed to being wet; after awhile they do not find this condition unpleasant, and later it is difficult to get them used to the idea of trying to stay dry.

If you observe your child lovingly, you will soon find out at which times elimination takes place. In many children, the bladder empties soon after the meal. Put the child on the pot at that time. If he was successful, praise the child— but no more than for any other accomplishment. If he was not successful, do not let the child sit on the pot too long, otherwise he will begin to play and will fail to realize why he is sitting there. The child should not "sit" longer than ten minutes. If he has had a bowel movement, take the child off the pot immediately, so that he will observe that this is the end of the "session." Always put him down in the same place at regular times and always on the same pot. The child will gradually come to understand what you want him to do and in time will act accordingly.

In putting the child on the pot, always say the same word. Repeat this word as long as the child is sitting. In time, he will connect this event with the word and will signal his need by using this word. Be careful in your choice of this word. In using it, your child should not be offensive, even if he should "signal" in the presence of strangers. If your child does not talk yet and if there is still no hope that he will learn to say a word after you, use one of the syllables that describes this activity in baby talk. This is better than certain hand movements that are not nice and that outsiders may find offensive. Train your child to indicate his need quietly, not by screaming or jumping up and down excitedly.

Once the child has made his need known, you must help immediately, because these children cannot wait. It is unfair to wait until the inevitable has happened and then reprove the child. This also interferes with the development of good habits.

The selection of the pot is important. There are children's chairs which have a small pot attached to the seat. These chairs are not suitable for retarded children. It is too difficult for them to understand that there are things that must be done in this chair at certain times that are absolutely forbidden at other times. It is better to put the child on a pot used exclusively for this purpose.

The pot should have a rather wide rim and should fit the child as well as possible, so that he will be able to sit on it comfortably. Some children have an aversion to the pot: they do not like to come into contact with the cold rim. In this case, we can heat the pot before use by pouring a little warm water in it.

Today we have baby seats that can be attached to a toilet bowl. In this manner, the child can use the ordinary toilet much sooner and the transition to the use of the standard toilet is facilitated. Of course, retarded boys can and should in time learn to urinate while standing.

The retarded child must not relieve himself anywhere except in the toilet or on his pot. If you make your child relieve himself in your yard because it is difficult to run into the house with the child, he will not be able to distinguish between a "suitable" and an "unsuitable" place. It is better to train the child to relieve himself only in the toilet. You will certainly not want your retarded child to be offensive.

Train the child to leave the toilet only after he has put his clothing in order again. Do not allow him to enter the room with his pants down or fly open—even if no one else happens to be there. Otherwise your child will show himself in an exposed condition in other places where he will not only be offensive but where he will also be in danger; this may have fateful consequences in future years. As long as the child cannot get himself buttoned up again, train him to call you when he needs help. Go to the toilet and arrange his clothing there. Don't have him come to you in the living room when incompletely dressed; he will be picking up a bad habit this way.

While the child is still in the wetting stage, he will have to wear diapers and rubber pants. This may also be necessary at a later stage when the child runs around freely. The child who walks around with wet diapers and rubber pants is much more liable to get a bad case of diaper rash than the infant who does not yet use his legs for locomotion. We must watch out for this and keep using baby powder and baby ointment long beyond the age for which these items are intended. Cleanliness is particularly important in an older child, not only for his own sake but also for the sake of other people. Nothing revolts acquaintances and strangers more than the child with an unpleasant odor.

Diapers and rubber pants must be considered a necessary evil; we must get the child to a point where he will no longer need them. These items do save us and our children from unpleasant situations, but at the same time they are a hindrance to toilet training. The mother pays less attention to the child's elimination as long as the visible results remain hidden; in turn, the child is less aware of the need for self-control. Many children make definite progress when diapers and rubber pants are discontinued, but we cannot hurry that time. It takes much empathy and a lot of common sense to make the decision as to whether the child still needs these items or whether he can do without them. Though the child may get along without them during the day, it is entirely possible that we may have to diaper him at night for a long time to come. This is true for most children.

Only when the child no longer wears diapers during the day can we get him to keep his clothes in order in connection with elimination. Girls are relatively faster in learning how to rearrange their clothing without help, because little pants with elastic are comparatively easy to handle.

Fortunately we also have pants with elastic for little boys. The trouble starts all over again when the boy begins to wear "real" pants. Here we must have much more patience with boys than with girls, because boys' clothing is much harder to handle. Buttoning his trousers may be too much for a boy, even if he can button his other clothing quite nicely. In this case it is better to replace the buttons with a zipper, in order to enable him to be on his own.

How long and to what extent your child needs your help depends not only on your efforts but also on the degree of his retardation. Even small forward steps toward the control of his needs and toward self-care help along the child's overall personality. As a result, the child is more readily acceptable to the family and fits into it more easily.

25

How Far Will the Child Get?

IF A DOCTOR tells you that your child is mentally retarded, your first question is probably: "Is it *serious?*" Again and again you ask yourselves and the specialist to whom you take the child whether this is a "light" case or whether the child is "untrainable." Every conscientious specialist will answer such questions in a more or less evasive manner. Perhaps you become angry because nobody "wants to give it to you straight." Perhaps you reproach doctors and counselors because they won't tell you "what it really is with the child."

This is not surprising. Doctors, psychologists, special educators, and education counselors are not prophets. The more experience they have, the less they will be inclined to make predictions as to how and how far a certain child will develop—least of all if the child is not even five years old. Everyone's future is uncertain—so is that of the retarded child.

During the first years, we cannot even remotely anticipate the developmental possibilities of a retarded child.

Evaluations based on appearance are deceptive. Even the mentally retarded child is sometimes pretty, with a friendly and perhaps even bright look, and one cannot always readily tell that his or her development is retarded. On the other hand, there are children who look so unfavorable that one is almost resigned to their fate from the beginning. But even among these we find children who develop beyond all expectation.

This is often true of Mongoloids. There are those among them whose degree of mental retardation does not correspond to their physical deformation; that is, they look worse than they are in reality. The more or less pronounced formation of the well-known Mongoloid characteristics does not allow us to arrive at any reliable conclusion as to the degree of mental retardation.

Children with cerebral palsy (including those suffering from Little's disease) also often have an unfavorable look. Their uncontrolled movements, deficient speech, drooling, expressionless faces—all these indicate a degree of mental retardation that is not present in many of them. About half of them have normal intelligence, but the disease prevents them from expressing this intelligence properly. The most hopeless-looking children often make astonishing improvement.

Progress here depends to a great extent on the care, perseverance, and consistency of the mother. In these children, daily practice of movements must be started during the first months. A doctor or experienced physiotherapist is best equipped to say which exercises are most suitable in each case. Large children's hospitals have diagnostic clinics and doctors specializing in the treatment of this disease. But it is not until the child is several years old that we can determine whether the disease has affected mental development or whether the child's intelligence is in line with his age.

A child who has attacks will probably develop less well than a child who does not have them. It is important to have these attacks eliminated through medical treatment; this will have an effect on the general future outlook.

A retarded child with a serious physical handicap does not have as good prospects as a child who can move properly. On the other hand, a physical handicap can be compensated for to some extent through persistent exercise. The extent to which we can be successful here depends not only on the paralysis but also on the mental development possibilities of the child. We cannot determine the latter in advance.

It is generally known today that we can determine an IQ with the help of tests. There are parents who insist on having their children tested in the hope that the results will give them information on the child's condition. Unfortunately we cannot measure intelligence as simply and reliably as, for instance, height or weight. We cannot really give an IQ test, as such, in the case of very young and greatly retarded children. But even if we can give such tests, the results do not tell us much. It takes years of living and working with the child to determine whether his capacities are particularly low or whether they are higher than expected.

The physician or psychologist can determine the child's status at a particular time, but he cannot determine future development trends on the basis of an examination. In general, the development of retarded children tends to slow down in time. The parents' hope that the child "will some day see the light" is therefore unfounded. The rate of development in general tends to slow down. Despite this generally valid finding, now and then there are children who can catch up in their development up to a point, especially if they learn to use what little they have in a purposeful and meaningful manner.

How far your child can develop depends not only on your care, your devotion, and your patience. There are seriously retarded children who never advance far enough to learn how to do things for themselves—not to speak of doing things for others. These children must be cared for and attended to as long as they live. On the other hand, there are those who in time learn not only how to take care of themselves but who also earn satisfaction and a place in society through useful work. And there are those whose development lies somewhere between these extremes.

No one can predict in advance to which category your child will belong. Do not, therefore, lose your perseverance; never despair. With this attitude, you will often be surprised by the progress your child makes. Nothing is more beautiful for parents to see than the way their child develops—even if progress is very slow.

Try hard to develop your child's existing capacities and do not mourn those he does not have. Try to help him achieve the degree of independence he is capable of. Try to train the child in such a manner that he will be borne along as far as possible by the rest of the family and by friends.

Your efforts will be richly rewarded. There is a world of difference between a well-trained, well-behaved retarded child and a child who was considered hopeless from the beginning and whose progress was given up. No child should ever be given up. Don't say: "Mental retardation is incurable. There is no use trying." This is not true! It is worthwhile to make every possible effort with any child. And if the future should really look dark, this is all the more reason to give the child a richer present.

26

Who Can Help?

You ARE NOT alone in your concern for your retarded child. First of all, you must take the child to a doctor. Only he can judge whether your little one can be helped with medication.

In addition, public health or welfare agencies can be of great assistance. Most communities have mental-retardation clinics in large hospitals or at a university teaching hospital. The state department of public health or mental hygiene can direct you to the clinic nearest your home.

Some parents are reluctant to approach an agency for advice. It is not the worst parents who shy away from accepting help. These agencies are not only for the poor, but for every social level. If financial troubles are piled on top of all the sorrow and worry about a child's development, the experienced case worker can, in many instances, help find the necessary funds.

Other parents fear that their child will not be theirs any more, once they have called in an agency. This fear is unfounded. No agency forces anyone to do anything. The case worker may, however, offer advice as to the measures that would help the child and as to the extent to which these measures are practicable. The case worker may specialize in retarded children (and adults), and therefore knows which possibilities and facilities should be considered in a particular case. If parents disagree between themselves as to the measures to be taken, an objective discussion with an outsider can have a good effect.

When your child is far enough advanced so that he will need more help that you can offer him at home, the case worker may give you the names of institutions established for the well-being of mentally retarded children.

For slightly retarded children, many communities have special classes forming a part of the public primary schools. But the seriously retarded whom we discuss in this book often cannot be admitted to these classes because they cannot keep up.

There are also special schools for these trainable retarded children. I have been directing such a school in the city of Zurich in Switzerland for the last twenty-five years. The hundreds of parents who have brought their children to me have shown me, on the one hand, the sorrows that weighed on them, and on the other, the astonishing success they have been able to achieve through tireless, daily training of their retarded children. The many years I have been working with their children have shown the general public that these children, too, can be and must be helped along in small groups. On the basis of the experience of our Zurich institution, other special schools for trainable children were set up in various places. Today we have such schools all over the world, many of them in the United

States. Some of these also have kindergarten sections. Most of these schools do not charge any tuition; some charge a small amount. In these schools, every child is developed to the extent permitted by his condition.

Besides, there are many residential schools for mentally retarded children throughout every country. These homes not only care for the children but also seek to educate them. Most have classroom activities in which the children are taught as much as they can learn. Homes that do not have such class hours keep the children busy in line with their capacities. There are parochial and public homes; private, public, and state homes. Which of the many residential institutions is the best for a certain child depends on the characteristics of the child and the attitude of the parents and family. If necessary, the local youth welfare offices and youth guidance centers cooperate in the financing.

This brings us to the question of whether a mentally retarded child should be brought up in the family or in a children's home. There is no generally valid answer to this. It depends both on the child and on the parents.

One cannot put a child away in an institution and act as if the child did not exist. Parents can never really forget their child. The more hopeless the child, the greater their sorrow, the greater their concern for the child. Nevertheless, it may happen that placement in a residential school is advisable.

Perhaps the child is so seriously impaired that his physical care alone will be beyond the mother's capabilities. Perhaps he is so overactive and unpredictable that he cannot be left alone for even a moment and never—even for a short time—in the care of anyone but his mother. In such cases, it is better to entrust the child to a residential institution so that the mother will not be so worn out that she is unable to take care of the rest of the family. Unfortunately there are very few homes that take such children; we must anticipate a long waiting period. Institutionalization may also be recommended if the mother has poor health or is unequal to the task for any other reason.

But if the child is happy in his own home—if he more or less fits into the family unit and does not constitute any insurmountable problem—we can keep him at home. No children's home can furnish the love and protection of a good family environment.

On the other hand, such institutions have a greater capability for helping a mentally retarded child than many a family home. The retarded child should live in a world in which he is not despised or rejected. He should have a chance to find friends who are on his own level, with whom he can compete, and whom he might even surpass in some respects. This is more likely in a children's home than in today's usual home life of the average small family.

Some parents balk at the idea of putting their child in an institution housing children who are obviously more retarded than their child. They want the child to be with children who are better off. They are not doing their child a favor in wanting this. It does not help the child's character to have to live in a group in which he is always the last.

In deciding whether or not a child is to be placed in a residential institution, one must also consider whether there is a nearby educational facility that the child can attend or whether he will be entirely dependent on the stimulation of his parents.

In some places, kindergarten teachers are willing to let a retarded child attend kindergarten on certain weekdays. This is of inestimable value to the child, even if he is past kindergarten age. But of course no kindergarten is obligated to take a retarded child; this is not its basic mission.

If there is a children's home nearby, a child can in some cases be accepted as a day student and can participate in training activities at certain times of the day.

Finally, there also might be an available teacher or private kindergarten school willing to care for your retarded child by the hour. But this is generally a very expensive solution and cannot replace the good effect of having your child be with other children.

27

Help Yourselves!

Do NOT ASK, full of bitterness: "Why has the public not done more for these children?" The answer is very simple: the public did not know about this plight. And how should it have known? The problem of mental retardation is as old as mankind, but until recently we have not talked about it. Those who are most concerned with it—parents—talk least about it, and if they do, then only in whispers. They lock the fact in their hearts and quietly wait for someone else to do something for their child. But how should others know how heavy your heart is—what you want for your children, what you need, and what your children need—if you keep concealing your plight and trying to embellish the situation?

The blind had their Helen Keller and many other famous people. The deaf had Beethoven and other outstanding personalities. Among retarded persons, there is none who, through his achievements, could demonstrate to the public his value and the value of those similarly afflicted. It is up to us, then, to uphold the value of these human beings. It is up to us to help extend respect for human dignity to these creatures also. It is up to us who live with them and who love them. We know what they need and what they can give us.

There is not one among the retarded whose worth is revealed to mankind as a tall, burning flame, reaching upward—like those great personalities who overcame their handicaps. Despite all our efforts, the retarded will always remain small flames. We must shield these little flames with our hands, as He did of Whom it was said: "The bent reed he will not break and the smoldering wick he will not extinguish." (Isaiah 42: 3.) For these miniature flames radiate warmth and soothing, quiet joy; they shine on the road that leads to the wisdom of the heart, to human maturity, and to true wealth.

You parents of retarded children have a mission that is greater than that of the care of your child. *Your* children guide you to a definite form of development.

The first stage you go through is the subjective, I-centered stage. This is the time during which your child's condition becomes manifest to you. In deep despair, you ask: "Why did this have to happen to *me?*" and: "What is this terrible event going to do to *my* life?" It appears that the gift you received in the person of your child brings, not joy, but deep sorrow. You find you have a cross to bear. The tears you shed are more for yourselves than for the child who peacefully and contentedly sleeps his baby sleep or lives a twilight childhood without suspecting what grief his existence is causing his parents.

The second stage of your growth comes when you begin to think less of yourselves and more of the child. This is the time when you ask who could help the child, who could assist you in training him. You find out that you do not know how to take care of your child, how to go about training him properly. In the past, this was not your problem. Now you realize that you are completely unprepared for a job you must do, a job that seems immense to you—and rightfully so. In this state, you went to the doctor. These and other questions made you pick up this book. This is understandable. You must get the best possible help for your child; you yourselves must seek the knowledge and skills that will enable you to offer your child the best.

But you should not be content with this: you can do better. In time, your concern for your own child should grow into concern for all handicapped children. This means that you should try to think more about what you can do for others and less about what others can do for your child. Experience has shown that the life of the parents is enriched by their retarded child if the parents feel some responsiblity for all such children. Self-pity—the worst of all emotional poisons—disappears as we develop a readiness to embrace warmly all those who need shelter. Then the cross we bear can become a blessing for others, and at the same time, for us.

Alone, two parents cannot do much. Left to themselves, they will have to be glad if they can manage to bring their own sorrow under control. But you are not alone with your child of sorrow; many parents have the same concern.

Groups of them have joined together to help each other. In many countries all over the world there are associations of parents of retarded children. Every state of the United

States has such associations, with many hundreds of local chapters. They are united in the National Association for Retarded Children, NARC, New York City (386 Park Avenue South). In Canada, there are over 200 local associations across the country. The headquarters of the Canadian Association for Retarded Children, CARC, is in Toronto, Ontario (87 Bedford Road). In the different countries of Europe there are altogether almost 100 such parents' associations. They are united in the International League of Societies for the Mentally Handicapped, in London (5 Bulstrode Street, W 1).

In some countries, groups of parents informed the public about the problem of mental retardation. They were instrumental in getting various countries to set up public institutions for mentally retarded individuals—an effort that is still under way. In other areas, where there were no facilities or where facilities were inadequate, parents themselves did what they felt was necessary. This included setting up schools or day-care centers, sheltered workshops for the handicapped, or vacation camps, and arranging discussion meetings for parents and recreation programs for retarded adolescents and adults.

Of course you have understanding relatives, friends, and neighbors. Still, you feel that these individuals share your sorrow to only a very limited degree. It is a great relief to talk to someone who really understands what goes on in your heart. The opportunity of talking to other parents and discussing similar problems gives you renewed incentive for your difficult task. It also gives you insight into the worries and concerns of others. Perhaps the lessons you learn can be helpful to other parents. Perhaps you will find that you have overestimated your own problem. By the time you read this book, one of these parents' associations may have set up a local chapter near your home.

You parents are charged with the mission of sharing, bearing, and shaping the very special fate of your child. If you break as you face this mission, you will also jeopardize your child's development. But if you grow with this mission, forces will be released within you that will enable you to give your child a richer life. If day in, day out, you do your best for your child, you can look to the future with confidence.

You are not alone with your child of sorrow. We parents are not our children's sole shelter. It would truly be bad for them if we were. Over us all stands the Protector of All Life. If we commend our children to Him, we will find that He has traced a path for every mother's child: healthy or ill, blossoming or retarded, richly endowed or dull.

GEORGE ALLEN & UNWIN LTD

London: 40 Museum Street, W.C.1

Auckland: P.O. Box 36013, Northcote Central, N.4
Bombay: 15 Graham Road, Ballard Estate, Bombay 1
Barbados: P.O. Box 222, Bridgetown
Buenos Aires: Escritorio 454–459, Florida 165
Calcutta: 17 Chittaranjan Avenue, Calcutta 13
Cape Town: 68 Shortmarket Street
Hong Kong: 105, Wing On Mansion, 26, Hancow Road, Kowloon
Ibadan: P.O. Box 62
Karachi: Karachi Chambers, McLeod Road
Madras: Mohan Mansions, 38c Mount Road, Madras 6
Mexico: Villalongin 32–10, Piso, Mexico 5, D.F.
Nairobi: P.O. Box 4536
New Delhi: 13–14 Asaf Ali Road, New Delhi 1
Ontario: 81 Curlew Drive: Don Mills
Rio de Janeiro: Caixa Postal 2537–Zc–00
São Paulo: Caixa Postal 8675
Singapore: 36c Prinsep Street, Singapore 7
Sydney, N.S.W.: Bradbury House, 55 York Street
Tokyo: P.O. Box 26, Kamata

CHILDREN AS NATURALISTS

MARGARET M. HUTCHINSON   *Cr. 8vo*

The aim of this new and much revised edition of CHILDREN AS NATURALISTS is to show teachers and parents how children's interest in Nature as part of Natural Science may be developed along true scientific lines embodying that sense of wonder and appreciation of beauty that needs cultivating in these days of emphasis on materialism and technology.

"Learning by doing" is as applicable to Nature as to most subjects and a child-centred school will encourage learning through channels that are natural to children: exploration and intimate contact with living things.

So, along these lines Part I discusses activities for different age groups and Part II describes aspects of Nature in the form of various quests: "The Quest for Birds", "The Quest for Fungi", etc. It also deals with the elements of Ecology and how the principles put forward in this book may be applied to town schools.

Miss Margaret Hutchinson is the grand-daughter of the late Sir Jonathan Hutchinson, F.R.S., surgeon, who founded the Educational Museum at Haslemere. Educated at the Friends' School, Sidcot, she later took the Teachers' Certificate of the National Froebel Foundation.

For twenty-five years she was principal of Yafflesmead Kindergarten and Junior School where, amid acres of garden, meadow and woodland, she built up with the children the happy contacts with nature which led to the writing of this and other books. Since 1955 when the school was given up, Miss Hutchinson has written a number of nature books for children. She serves on committees of the National Froebel Foundation and The School Natural Science Society, and has written articles and leaflets for these educational bodies. Her holidays are spent bird-watching as far afield as Australia and New Zealand.

EMOTIONAL DISORDERS OF CHILDREN

GERALD H. J. PEARSON   *Demy 8vo*

"An important volume for all students of psychiatry." *British Journal of Delinquency*

INFANTS WITHOUT FAMILIES

DOROTHY BURLINGHAM, ANNA FREUD

Cr. 8vo

Originally published in 1944, this book has become a standard work on the problem of the young child without a home of his own. In her Foreword to this edition, Miss Freud explains that the passage of time has made no fundamental change in their evaluation of the advantages of residential life in an Institute at different phases and in different aspects of the infant's development. They come to the conclusion that there are realms in the infant's life where the residential nursery can be helpful by creating excellent conditions for certain types of development; but that there are others where residential homes have to recognize their limitations if they want to face and fight more effectively the serious consequences of such limitations.

The observations recorded in this book provide a valuable contribution towards discussion of the question: Should residential nurseries be maintained, and if so, can they be changed so as not to produce the "institutional" child?

Comparison between psychological development under family and residential conditions touches on many important aspects of the infant's life.

PLAYTIME IN THE FIRST FIVE YEARS

HILARY PAGE

Demy 8vo

'Even when the author delves into the realms of psychology there is no complexity of language and the fundamental desires which motivate a child's play are straightforwardly expounded."
The Yorkshire Observer

DELINQUENCY AND CHILD NEGLECT

HARRIETT WILSON   *Demy 8vo*

This is the first comprehensive study of a group of families often referred to as "problem families." Harriett Wilson shows that they are not a homogeneous group, and furthermore, that they do not possess any unique personality traits. On the contrary, the disabilities which are found among the families who took part in this investigation are also found in the general run of the population. The main disabling factor turned out to be the social isolation to which these families are subjected.

This isolation affects not only the personality of father and mother but it has also a profound effect on the character formation of their children, who tend to become delinquent. The child from this environment has not learnt to control his impulses effectively enough to take part in social life on a normal basis. He is handicapped from an early age.

Harriett Wilson concludes that the delinquency found in this environment is a symptom of a total family situation which can only be treated at the family level by preventative family services.

"This is a lively and stimulating book and is well worth reading by every teacher in a densely populated area." *Education*

"A valuable and careful sociological study . . . not only a solid but an attractive study." *New Society*

ON EDUCATION

BERTRAND RUSSELL   *Cr. 8vo*

"His quick intelligence makes him lucid, able in statement, and so gently acid in his humour that we hardly realize the destruction of our favourite parental sentimentalities." *The Observer*

NO TWO ALIKE

D. M. DYSON *La. Cr. 8vo*

The care of children deprived of normal home life is a national problem. All who pay rates or subscribe towards the work of the voluntary child care societies accept some measure of responsibility, willingly or unwillingly.

Foster parents, and those who could be foster parents but are not, those who recommend foster parents and those who could promote fostering but do not, all have their share of responsibility in helping or failing to help.

Members of local authority children's committees and councils of voluntary services employ residential staff in homes and child care officers, and they have to make decisions for individual children; they need to understand as fully as possible the problems in the homes and the individual and time-consuming work of the child care officers. Residential staff and child care officers accept their share in this enthralling and responsible work.

This book will help towards deeper understanding for it is written out of the experience of one worker who has tried to see below the surface, and to be guided not too much by generalizations and by current theories, but by consideration of how each individual child can best be helped.

A NEW INTRODUCTION TO PSYCHOLOGY

JOHN COHEN *Demy 8vo*

This book has been prepared as an up-to-date text for those who wish to begin a serious study of psychology either within the natural or the social sciences. It provides a general introduction to the basic problems, methods and contributions of contemporary psychology and devotes several chapters to the psychological foundations of educational practice—in the study of child development, learning and remembering, thinking and communicating. It should therefore prove especially suitable for students in Colleges of Education. Adequate references are given for the student who wishes to pursue any particular topic, and guidance is given for further reading.

GEORGE ALLEN AND UNWIN LTD